NO CAUSE FOR PANIC

Cover: Channel Islands refugees awaiting train to go north.

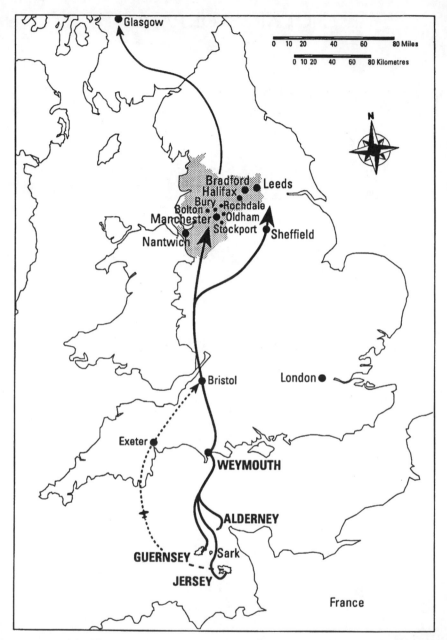

Evacuation of the Channel Islands: The main routes of the 30,000 evacuees in June 1940. A large majority disembarked at Weymouth from where they were taken north on special trains. About 400 travelled by air to Bristol (with a refuelling stop at Exeter). Many remained until 1945-6 in Lancashire, Cheshire and the West Riding, particularly in the towns shown in the shaded area.

NO CAUSE FOR PANIC

Channel Islands Refugees, 1940-45

Brian Ahier Read

SEAFLOWER BOOKS

Published in 1995 by
SEAFLOWER BOOKS
16 and a half New St. John's Road
St. Helier
Jersey

Seaflower Books is an imprint of Ex Libris Press,
to whom all enquiries and correspondence
should be addressed:

EX LIBRIS PRESS
1 The Shambles
Bradford on Avon
Wiltshire
BA15 1JS

Typeset in 10 point Palatino

Design and typesetting by Ex Libris Press
Cover printed by Shires Press, Trowbridge, Wiltshire
Printed and bound by
Cromwell Press, Broughton Gifford, Wiltshire

ISBN 0 948578 69 6

Contents

Acknowledgements

Channel Islands evacuees were scattered widely in Britain during the war and the Local Studies Departments of some libraries in the UK have documents relating to one of the CI Societies or other material arising from the temporary stay of the refugees in their areas. I am grateful to the many librarians who have searched their collections on my behalf. In particular I should like to acknowledge the help I received from Mrs P. Godman of Rochdale library, Kevin Mulley, the Archivist for Bury, and Bill Gallienne of Guernsey Archives. Sally Knight of the Lord Coutanche library of the Société Jersiaise was most helpful at a time when the work of the library was disrupted by building operations. Special thanks are also due to Freda Millett and Peter Fox of Oldham Museum for allowing me access to the exhibits from the 'Guernsey Boys' exhibition held in 1990.

I am indebted to a number of people who have supplied information or allowed me to quote from published memoirs: firstly members of the Cox family, particularly Mrs Audrey Wilson and Stanley Wilson, for giving me access to the letters of the late Mrs Cox and tape recordings of family memories of 1940. Then to Mrs Elizabeth Downer and Anne Nichol for allowing me to quote at length from the diary of their mother, the late Mrs Diana Nichol (née Falla). Also to Mrs Betty Fooks for allowing me to quote from *X-Iles*, the wartime autobiography of her father, Edward Hamel, and to Olive Quin for quotations from her book *The Long Goodbye*. Mr V. G. Collenette kindly allowed me to quote from his history *Elizabeth College in Exile* and Mr Michael Marshall from *The Small Army*.

I am also grateful to the following who have sent me documents or reminiscences, either their own or notes made by their parents about their experiences of the evacuation: John Bennett, Molly Bihet, Anne G. Bissell Thomas, W.A. Bisson, Margaret Brehaut, Janet Castle, Yvonne Coppock, Ken Craven, W.W. Hammond, A.R. Keeling, John Lainé, Brian Le Messurier, Margaret Le Page, Leslie C. Le Tocq, Sheila Marquand, Betty M. Moore, Margaret Newman, Kenneth Renault, Fay Robinson, Barbara Steer, Nancy R. Tonkin, Richard Walker, G.V. Williams.

Some of my correspondents may be disappointed at not finding their individual stories and comments in the following pages. I hope they will accept my apologies and assurance that all their material was most helpful in throwing light on the difficulties, dilemmas and hardships of the evacuees.

Illustrations

Introduction

No period of Channel Island history has had so many books written about it as the German occupation of 1940-45. They usually begin with the evacuation of June 1940 before focusing on events in the islands. Little has been written about the experiences of the 30,000 people, including 4,000 schoolchildren without their parents, who, after a sudden decision to leave home, found themselves in wartime England with few possessions, little or no money and no idea of where they would live.

This book is an attempt to fill that gap. It tells how the evacuees were helped by the British public and how they adapted to new lives, often in surroundings quite different in character from the environment they had been used to.

After the war a few of the evacuees wrote about their experiences and a small number of these reminiscences have been published. Although I have quoted from personal stories whenever it seemed that an individual's comment added colour or useful detail, I have tried to tell the story on a broader canvas, using official records and contemporary reports.

During my researches I have sometimes been asked whether I was an evacuee myself in 1940. At that time I was a schoolboy in Jersey and with my family I remained in the island throughout the Occupation. Perhaps this was why I embarked on this book: I was curious to know what life might have been like if my family had evacuated.

Brian Ahier Read
Henley on Thames
February 1995

Chapter 1

Evacuation

Well, when we saw the clouds of smoke in the sky from the Germans blowing up things across the water in France, and boatloads of French came over with horrible stories of what the Germans was doing to them, I reckon we all knew our turn was coming. There was some fools who thought the Germans wouldn't bother about little Guernsey; but I have never been one to hope for the best when the worst is staring me in the face. The question everybody was asking was whether to stop in Guernsey or stop in England. That is, if they could. One minute it was said everybody would have to go; and the next minute that nobody would be able to. Then nobody could make up their minds if they wanted to or not.

from *The Book of Ebenezer Le Page* by G.B. Edwards

Paris surrendered to the Germans on 14 June 1940. British and French troops had escaped from St. Malo, on the French coast south of the Channel Islands, by 18 June.

Early in June 1940 the public of the Channel Islands seemed remarkably unruffled. Daily newspapers in both Jersey and Guernsey continued to report war news as if the islands were far removed from the scenes of battle. Guernsey's *Evening Press* carried an advertisement right up to 18 June inviting readers to 'Spend your holidays in the Channel Islands' and listing hotels in Jersey and Sark. The daily ferries from Southampton continued to carry passengers to Guernsey and Jersey.

In London military chiefs decided by Saturday 15 June that the islands were of no strategic importance and could not be defended. But communication between the British government and the island governments was muddled. The official historian of the Occupation Charles Cruickshank commented later that the 'demilitarisation and partial evacuation were so clumsily handled that had the facts been known to the British people at the time it would have weakened their faith in the government's ability to win the war.'

The civil heads of the four main islands each acted in a different way; to a large extent it was their attitudes that shaped the course of events and resulted in people staying in their island home or fleeing to England.

9

In Jersey, although arrangements were made for a voluntary evacuation, the Bailiff, Alexander Coutanche, said firmly that people should stay.

In Guernsey there was some dithering but a speedy decision was made to evacuate children. In Sark the Dame, Mrs Sibyl Hathaway, who in her younger days had lived and worked in Germany, had no intention of leaving. In Alderney Judge French sought advice from Guernsey and, getting none, asked the British government to send a ship to evacuate the residents.

It is also likely that the headlines on the main newspapers of Guernsey and Jersey of 19 June strongly influenced some people when they first saw them. News of the demilitarisation and a possible evacuation of the islands was announced on that day. EVACUATION OF CHILDREN was spread across the front page of the *Guernsey Press* of 19 June.

In Jersey the *Evening Post* of the same day was more subdued. In an inside page there was a single column headline:

GRAVE DECISION
ISLAND TO BE DEMILITARISED

Jersey's firm lead

The Lieutenant-Governor had told the States of Jersey in the afternoon that the evacuation of British forces from France was now complete and that he was already sending British troops out of the island. He said that the British government hoped to evacuate the bulk of those who wished to go but he felt sure that those who had their roots in the soil would not want to leave.

In the *Evening Post* that evening was a short notice which was clearly provided by an official source but not signed or attributed. It was headed EVACUATION:

> Shipping facilities are being provided by His Majesty's Government for the immediate voluntary evacuation to the United Kingdom of women and children. Similar facilities will also be available for men between the ages of 20 and 33 who wish to join His Majesty's Forces and, so far as accommodation permits for other men.
>
> The names and addresses of all women and children (and of all such men other than persons for whom tickets have already been bought from the Southern Railway) should be handed in at the special office at the Town Hall before 10 o'clock tonight, Wednesday June the 19 or between 6 a.m. and 10 a.m. tomorrow, Thursday...
>
> Information will in the case of women and children be required to be given as to whether arrangements have been, or will be made privately, for the accommodation and maintenance in the United

Kingdom or whether accommodation and maintenance should be provided for them by the appropriate United Kingdom authorities.

The 19 June was described by the diarist Leslie Sinel as 'a day of wild rumour' and, he added, 'the suddenness of the decision flung the Island into a panic.'

A long queue of people waiting to register for the evacuation formed at the Town Hall. It moved slowly towards desks where several clerks listed names and addresses but by 10 p.m. there was still a huge number of people waiting and they were told to go home and come back in the morning. The queue had been orderly and only four policemen were on duty to control it.

Although officially this was a voluntary evacuation, some thought it was compulsory. Nan Le Ruez's diary entry for 19 June records, 'Everybody upset. Jersey States have ordered evacuation…people all in a panic.'

She joined the Town Hall queue at 5.30 the next morning and after standing all day registered at 6.30 in the evening, but that night wrote in her diary, '…after much thought and prayer, I felt it was silly to go off in a panic. Better wait…' And she remained in the island.

Guy Porter, who lived at 24, Regent Road, St Helier, wrote to a friend a few days later: 'We were told on the 19th that all who wanted to leave must register at the Town Hall. Immediately there was a long queue. I went there at 4.40 the next morning and waited until 11 o'clock before I could register. I then went to the GPO and two of the banks but could not get near these places for the crowd.'

A baker's roundsman, George Bird, aged 20 at the time, remembers the 19th because it was the day his customers told him they wanted no more bread because they were leaving the island. After giving the bread away he joined the queue for the Town Hall but it was so long that he was in Gloucester Street (not far from the Opera House) at 8 p.m. and by 10 p.m. he had moved only a short distance. People in the queue were then told that the Town Hall was closing and would open again at five in the morning. He was there at 5 a.m. but the Town Hall did not open until 7 a.m. In the meantime, he says, Ned Le Quesne, who was a prominent member of the States, came along and was telling people they shouldn't leave the island.

"But can you guarantee we'll have food?" someone asked. Le Quesne replied, "No, I can't guarantee food but I can tell you that towns in England are being heavily bombed so I don't advise you to go there." George Bird could not remember anyone leaving the queue. He himself thought it would be 'a glorious adventure' to evacuate free of any charge.

F. Audley Harman, headmaster of the Jersey High School, Stopford Road, St Helier, also queued at the Town Hall on the evening of the 19th and then returned there at 4.30 the next morning, eventually registering at 11.15. He described the rest of the day in a diary written a few days later:

Collect ration books from Orviss [a grocery], queues at banks, shops closed. Take Kitty and Mick [dogs] to Animals' Shelter. Pay 2/6d

11

Above: Thousands queued at St Helier's Town Hall on 20 June 1940 to register for evacuation. Others filled the streets to watch, so adding to the confusion. Below: On 20 June 1940 people of all ages were waiting at St. Helier harbour for a free passage to England.

but were told one of the vets had had accident and it would take one and a half hours. Waited until 4.15 in boiling sun. Saw all sorts of dogs, large, small, gentle and quarrelsome. Hurried home. At 4.45 we all pile into car with luggage. Streets lined with abandoned cars. Queue on Great Western quay as wide as quay itself. We visualise another long wait but suddenly the queue about turns and we find ourselves almost at the front as the crowd makes for the Southern Railway pier. Soon, in about 15 minutes, we are through the barrier. We make our way along to a boat. On the way we see one boatload leaving, a low barge-like vessel quite unsuited to crossing more than an inland canal. We embark on a small collier, filthy, unprotected and overloaded (350 on board), no magnetic mine protection, no Lewis gun, no lifebelts, just one small lifeboat. Boat sails at 7 p.m. One mug for all on board. Sleep on iron deck-plates. Ships' crew very kind, engineer offers his cabin to mother with 5. Relief at seeing land (Isle of Wight). Stopped by destroyers, take on pilot, feel our way through minefield.

Mr Harman, with his wife and young children embarked in Southampton and were able to travel to relatives in Hove, Sussex. A few days after their arrival Mrs Harman wrote to her father who had remained in Jersey:

I am still completely at sea as to whether we really should have stayed. Everything was such a frightful nightmare those two days. I wish to God there had been more time to think before we came away…the authorities (English and Jersey) were at least partly to blame for the frightful muddle. Audley spent two hours at the Town Hall in the evening trying to register, and then from 4 a.m. to 11 the next morning and after all that we might just as well not have registered at all as nothing whatever was asked for. Just imagine that ghastly, panicky crowd on the quay and me with Rosemary in her Karricot, and as much of our belongings as we had managed to get into two small cases and a rucksack. I'd never even contemplated such a quandary in all my life.

Spectators on the Albert Pier, St. Helier, watching departure of evacuees on 21 June 1940.

Guernsey

In Guernsey events were unfolding rather differently. On 17 June a meeting of the Education Council (the States committee for education) was told that evacuation was a possibility and they agreed to support the evacuation of school children if it was recommended. The next day a meeting of all head teachers was held in the afternoon and they were told in confidence that evacuation of schoolchildren was possible and should be planned. A committee was elected consisting of two members of the council, four head teachers, (C.R. Stutchbury, C.J. Rawlinson, Miss A. Ninnim, Miss E.O. Robilliard), and the Secretary of the Council (A. Winterflood).

On the morning of 19 June the four heads and Mr Winterflood together drafted a letter to be sent to all parents but whilst they were doing this they were asked to go to the Royal Court at 11.00. Here were the island's leaders, including the Bailiff (Sir Victor Carey), H.M. Procureur (Major Ambrose Sherwill) and Jurat John Leale. They were told that a voluntary evacuation might take place within a few hours but they must not yet disclose this information to the public.

Meanwhile a Channel Islands envoy who had gone to London earlier in the week, Jurat Edgar Dorey of Jersey, had flown to Guernsey and reported to the Bailiff that the British government would announce demilitarisation and a voluntary evacuation of the islands.

Soon after 3.30 p.m. on 19 June a meeting of the teachers was told officially that an evacuation of the children had been decided. All children whose parents wished it were to be evacuated at once. Three ships from England would arrive during the night. Teachers were instructed to consult parents, asking them if they agreed to their children being sent away to an unknown destination and were given printed copies of a letter for parents. Registration would take place at each school from 7 p.m. that evening and teachers were to telephone the number registered as soon as possible. Almost all parents did agree, with the result that few Guernsey children were in the island during the German occupation which followed. The writer V.V. Cortvriend, in her book *Isolated Island*, written during the Occupation, likened the situation to that of Hamelin after the children had followed the Pied Piper.

During the afternoon and evening copies of the Guernsey broadsheet *Evening Press* were distributed with the headline across the whole of its front page

EVACUATION OF CHILDREN
PARENTS MUST REPORT THIS EVENING.

Many people, especially those in the rural parts of the island, had not read the official statements, or had misinterpreted them, and did not understand that the evacuation was voluntary. This caused widespread panic. Several farmers slaughtered their cattle unnecessarily. The High Street of St Peter Port was so crowded that people were fainting and members of St. John's Ambulance had to be called.

On the following day the *Evening Press* tried to calm the situation with the headlines:

NO CAUSE FOR PANIC
Run on Banks Must Stop
ADVICE TO CARRY ON AS USUAL

'The scenes in the town this morning will never be forgotten by any Guern-seyman,' reported the newspaper. 'Thousands thronged the narrow streets making last minute arrangements prior to evacuation.'

Many people who had registered in the belief that a ship would be immediately available arrived at the harbour on that Thursday morning with their luggage. A barrier prevented access to the quay and they were not given any information.

Throughout Thursday the evacuation of schoolchildren continued. John Bennett, who was an 11-year old pupil of the Lower School of Elizabeth College, remembers 19 June well because it was his father's birthday. He says, "We were told at school that we must go home and ask our parents for permission to

evacuate. When I got home there were several neighbours discussing the position with my father because they were so undecided as to what to do. My father agreed that I should go. Hardly anybody in my class was refused permission."

The next day John went to school with a packed suitcase. The boys waited until the middle of the afternoon in the grounds at the front of Elizabeth College. The weather was hot and calm. By this time they had had no food since breakfast so they were all sent home, leaving their suitcases at the College. When they returned they waited all the evening in the same place and at 10 p.m. they were told that they would board a ship soon. Two van drivers offered to take their luggage to the harbour and they marched with their teachers to the ship, a Dutch cargo vessel, the *Batavier IV*, three abreast.

By Friday 21 June the evacuation of school-children from Guernsey was virtually complete. Officials began to make efforts to calm the situation. The States had recently made Deputy Stamford Raffles responsible for information. On Saturday 22 June he had posters printed and distributed throughout the island.

These ran:

Keep your heads! Don't be yellow! Business as Usual!
Why go mad? Compulsory evacuation a lie.

There's no place like home. Cheer up!
The rumour that general evacuation
has been ordered is a lie!

On the same day a senior member of the States, Jurat the Rev. (later Sir) John Leale(1892-1969), addressed a crowd waiting near the harbour, advising them to go home. This speech and perhaps the posters persuaded some to change their minds and they decided not to leave the island. Exact figures of how many did evacuate were not recorded but it was estimated at the time that out of the population of 43,000, 20,000 went to England, including about 4,000 children mostly as school classes. The *Guernsey Press* reported on 8 July 1940 that 1,051 children of school age were left in the island.

Sark

The population of Sark at that time was 500, headed by the autocratic Dame of Sark, Mrs Sibyl Hathaway (1884-1974). In her autobiography written after the war she says that after the letter from the Home Office of 19 June telling the Bailiffs of Jersey and Guernsey that they should stay at their posts, 'I went over the Guernsey for the day to find out for myself what was happening there, and was appalled when I saw the panic...The States offices were in a state of utter confusion and the only man who appeared cool, calm and collected was the Bailiff's secretary.'

On her return to Sark she called a meeting of the inhabitants and told them that she would stay with her daughter and granddaughter but that transport to England could be arranged for those who wished to leave. 'I am not promising that it will be easy,' she told the assembly. 'We may be hungry but we will always have our cattle and crops, our gardens, a few pigs, our sheep and rabbits.'

She claimed that as a result of this meeting not one Sark-born person evacuated. The Seneschal, William Carré, toured the island asking for the names of anyone who wished to be evacuated but the response was small. A little later there was a telephone call from Guernsey asking if a boat was required and Mrs Hathaway is said to have replied to the effect that nobody wished to evacuate although after the war some claimed that they would have left if an evacuation boat had arrived. A few English residents left and on 24 June, the Dame wrote to a relative in London (Diana):

> All is calm here now. I was in Guernsey when all the panic started. So disgracefully run there. No one took any lead and explained. We have 471 people to feed here...

A few days later she wrote to the Home Office:

> No Sark native has left. Much panic was caused by the sudden news of evacuation. Guernsey authorities did not inform Sark till 7 p.m. on 19th that any children for evacuation should be registered by 7.30 am on the 20th and our medical officer behaved disgracefully and bolted, leaving no medical man for the island at all and making more panic.

Alderney

In June 1940 the population of this small and rather backward island, eight miles from the coast of France, numbered about 1,500. A British Army machine-gun training unit had been in Alderney for some months but on 16 June 1940 it was suddenly ordered to leave. This, and the fact that heavy gunfire could be seen and heard on the coast of France and distraught French refugees were arriving in small boats, caused some panic on the island.

The civil head of Alderney was at that time the senior jurat of the States of Alderney (referred to as 'Judge...'). A 50 year old retired colonial administrator and former soldier, Frederick George French (1889-1962) had been elected to this office in 1937.

Facilities to communicate with Guernsey and England were poor (the under-sea telephone cable was defective). Judge French sent a telegram to Guernsey asking for advice. The reply on 19 June, in effect, told him to do whatever he thought fit.

Various accounts of what happened in Alderney during the week beginning 17 June have been published. In the absence of firm advice from outside the island, French was placed in the difficult position of having to make a terrible decision: to evacuate or to stay.

On Friday 21 June the Trinity House ship Vestal arrived to take off the lighthouse personnel and their families. French asked the Captain, John Cecil McCarthy (1899-1947) to take a message to the Admiralty in which he asked for vessels to evacuate the inhabitants. Next morning, Saturday, he posted a hand-written notice on the Courthouse door which he had signed personally. This included:

I have appealed to the Admiralty for a ship to evacuate us.
If the ship does not come, it means we are considered safe.
If the ship comes, time will be limited.
You are advised to pack one suitcase for each person so as to be ready...

It is sometimes said that the whole population evacuated because they were advised to do so by Judge French. However some writers claim that the decision to leave was taken largely by a show of hands at an open-air meeting on Saturday 22 June after French had addressed them from the back of a lorry. After explaining the position he is reported to have ended by saying, "Do we go, or do we stay? Whatever we do, let's all do the same!"

At four the next morning six ships did arrive. The church bells rang and people steeled themselves to leave. Dogs were shot. Cattle, cats and other pets were turned loose. By noon almost everybody had left the island. In 1942 a survey of these refugees concluded that there were 1,432 people: 502 men, 529 women and 401 children.

Before they left the Island Judge French withdrew all the cash, amounting to £1,322. 17. 8d., from the Alderney banks and held it in the form of cash withdrawals on States accounts. The money, partly in English notes but mainly in Guernsey notes, was kept in the Captain's cabin on board the *Stork* and on arrival in Weymouth was handed to the police for safe keeping. After the evacuation it was agreed by the British government that the banks would exchange Guernsey notes until 23 July 1940 to a value of £50 for any one refugee. A letter from the Treasury dated 19 Dec 1940, referring to the £50 limit, said, 'We do not want people who find opportunities to escape bringing suitcases full of notes.' By the end of 1940 £27,548 was paid by the Home Office to the Bank of England.

In Weymouth the Alderney refugees who had nowhere to go were put on trains to be taken to the north. Many were received in Glasgow, where they were put into reception centres until they could be billetted or had found other accommodation. Meanwhile Judge French went to London where he continued to act as Alderney's representative. He was now sure that they had done the right thing in evacuating as is shown by his letter of thanks to McCarthy, dated 8 July 1940, which he signed as 'Yours most gratefully and sincerely on behalf of all the people of Alderney.' He wrote:

Now that the Island of Alderney has been completely evacuated and all but a handful of its people safely snatched out of the grip of the Boche, I write to thank you first and foremost on my own personal behalf and secondly in the name of all the people of the Island for your action in forwarding my request to the Ministry of Shipping and to the Admiralty. The present safety of us all is due entirely to your prompt action and to nothing else....

When you so readily and so kindly consented to act upon my request you lifted a great burden from my mind. When I was able to tell the people the following morning of your promise all apprehension and panic subsided and all of us waited in perfect faith for the result...

As you may know six vessels arrived in less than twenty hours.

Two days after the rush from Alderney a party of farmers from Guernsey went to the abandoned island and found dreadful scenes of a hurried and cruel departure. Only 12 people were there, including four children. Cattle, horses, pigs, cats and dogs were running loose but there were also animals in closed yards, unable to get food or water. Some calves were found tied up in stables, left to die of starvation.

A month later

Within a few weeks some of the evacuees, faced with the difficulties of starting a new life, felt that they had made the wrong decision in abandoning their homes. A Jersey businessman who wrote to the Home Office on 26 July 1940 seeking help said that Channel Islanders 'who are now in England are feeling very bitter about the whole thing. I have had to leave a very good business with approximately £7,000 due to me by the farmers and about £7,000 worth of stock.'

Many other people wrote to the Home Office asking for compensation for the property they had left in the islands. Their reply was a standard letter:

Sir/Madam, With reference to your letter of.........regarding your property in the CIs, I am directed by the Sec. of State to say that he regrets that the Government cannot undertake any liability in respect of such property and that no machinery exists for registering it. I am, Sir/Madam, Your obedient servant, A. Maxwell.

The Lieutenant Governor of Guernsey, Major General Minshull Ford asked the government in June to compensate him for the loss of 'family treasures.' His hand-written list was comprehensive and gave the total value as £1611. 9. 6d. It included 12 jam jars in the kitchen cupboard, a 12lb side of bacon, 1 cwt bar soap, 1 cwt soda and lavatory paper. He too was refused compensation.

There were strong criticisms in the British Parliament of the way the evacuation of the Channel Islands was conducted. During an adjournment debate in the House of Commons on 31 July the M.P. for Camberwell North, Mr Ammon said he had received 'a tremendous batch of letters.' He quoted one from an evacuee which said, 'So far from being 'voluntary' the evacuation was encouraged and ARP wardens went round imploring the people to get out before they were blown out. We were told that the Jerries would be here in 24 hours, the men would be taken to Germany as slaves in the munitions factories, and as for our women, well, God help them!' Ammon spoke very strongly, referring to 'muddle, vacillation and failure to realise the responsibilities of the position, to say nothing of the humiliation which every Britisher must feel because we walked out.'

A Grave Decision

A decision of the most vital importance to the island was taken today by the British Cabinet and announced to the States of Jersey this afternoon by His Excellency the Lieut.-Governor.

This island is not to be defended; it is to be completely demilitarised and declared an undefended zone. The reasons governing this decision are the concern of His majesty's Government, and we may rest assured that the most profound attention was given to every aspect before it was decided to take this step. We believe there to be no reason at all for panic; the government of the island will go on, and everything will be done to ensure the smooth working of the administration. Keep calm, obey the regulations issued by the authorities and carry on, as far as it is possible, with one's ordinary business. We believe we can offer no saner or sounder advice.

Evening Post, Jersey, 19 June 1940

30,000 people left the Channel islands abruptly in the eleven days before 30 June 1940. Over 20,000 crowded on to cargo vessels for a sea journey which lasted at least ten hours. Children travelling with their school classes were allowed to take only a small case or bundle. Adults were limited to 28 lbs. of luggage. Before they left many queued at banks but because of a cash shortage withdrawals were restricted to £20, about a month's income for an average worker.

Reginald Biddle

Chapter 2

Crossing the Channel

I have been associated with the services to the Channel Islands for 37 years. There have been many sad occasions during that period, but the most tragic were the arrangements under the voluntary evacuation scheme.

R. P. Biddle, 19 May 1941.

It was an uncomfortable sea journey because the ships which they were on were for the most part cargo vessels which had been in use for the transport of coal, flour, stone or other bulk materials. Most had little or no passenger accommodation. People had to lie on the open decks or in dusty holds for an overnight journey that lasted about twelve hours. Sometimes there were several hours delay as the ship waited to be berthed in Weymouth. They were fortunate however in two ways: the weather was warm and calm and none of the ships was attacked by the enemy.

It may also have been a lucky coincidence that the man in charge of Southampton Docks at that time, and therefore with important responsibilities for Channel Island shipping, was himself a Channel Islander. He was Reginald Poulton Biddle (1888-1970), a Jerseyman who was appointed Docks and Marine Manager, Southampton in 1936. Later in 1940 he was Deputy Director of Ports at the Ministry of War Transport. In 1944 he was awarded the CBE for his services in planning the Normandy landings.

In 1941 Biddle presented a paper to the Jersey Society in London in which he wrote:

The night of June 19th/20th was a busy one. Special and immediate measures had to be taken to send all available and suitable tonnage to the Channel Islands to bring away those who desired to leave. The whole of the resources of the Railway Company's staff and facilities were unreservedly placed at the disposal of the local authorities. Entirely on my own initiative I sent certain of the S.R. company's steamers to the islands. They had only peace-time certificates to carry 12 passengers but between them they brought over nearly 3,000 evacuees.

The evening of Wednesday June 19th in Jersey, and no doubt in

Guernsey, saw much chaos and confusion. The worst was expected at any moment. Indeed, I was told in a telephone message from Jersey at 10 o'clock that the Germans were expected to arrive the next morning, and what was I going to do about it?

I endeavoured to create an atmosphere of greater calm by the information that the steamers referred to above had already sailed.

My own staff in Jersey were not unnaturally anxious about their families and within an hour or two yet another steamer had been commissioned and had sailed for Jersey.

The number of telephone messages I received for news of people in Jersey and for particulars of the evacuation arrangement was astronomical!

June 20, 21 and 22 (Saturday) were the days when embarkation took place. On the Saturday there were steamers alongside the quays at Jersey but only a few evacuees presented themselves for embarkation, whereas at Guernsey there were literally thousands waiting at the harbour and insufficient vessels to deal with them.

Arrangements were made to make public announcements in the streets of St Helier, and by various other means, that ships were waiting at the quay, but in the late afternoon it was decided to send them to Guernsey where they were immediately besieged by waiting passengers.

It would appear that of nearly 20,000 who registered under the Jersey States evacuation scheme not more than 10,000 availed themselves of the facilities, whereas at Guernsey the original number of 13,000 registered quickly rose to 20,000, all of whom had been embarked by the Sunday night.

It was very desirable, in order to maintain an atmosphere of confidence in those who had decided to remain in the islands, for the mailboat service to and from the islands to be continued as long as circumstances permitted. This was the wish of the government on this side and the Southern Railway agreed on the understanding that they would be kept advised of developments. With great courage and a loyal sense of duty the staff in Jersey readily agreed to continue at their posts. It was a bitter disappointment that the subsequent march of events developed with such tragic suddenness that those splendid fellows were unable to leave the island. They set a fine example which will never be forgotten.

On the Saturday (22 June) after a conversation with the Home Office I spoke personally to the Bailiff of Jersey and to the Attorney General at Guernsey notifying that the mailboat services would continue, and statements to this effect were immediately announced in the States.

And so the services, both passenger and cargo, pursued their normal course until the end of the following week.

Biddle's mention of the loyal behaviour of the staff in the Southern Railway offices was supported later by a young Jerseyman, Mr McLennan-Jones, who was working in the Guernsey office of the Great Western & Southern Railway in June 1940. He wrote:

> All the staff were told they could go on the *Isle of Sark* but when they got to the White Rock there was a big crowd expecting to get aboard the *Duke of York*, another evacuation boat. However this was to be used only for children under school age and their mothers so it was decided that the GW staff would help with the boarding of the mothers and children. The captain of the *Duke of York* said he could take 1,200 people and ordered that we should count them as they went aboard. Some of the staff helped to carry the baggage and the children up the gangways but as the tide rose these got steeper and more difficult. Many of the children were wailing in alarm and as soon as they were set down in the saloon started running around looking for their mothers. As the morning wore on, the ship was in an uproar, children crying, running around, being sick, yelling for food, or just yelling.
>
> At about 10.30 the captain arrived and checked the number loaded. It was about 1,000 and he insisted we stop at 1,200. Even then the line of buses full of children stretched right up the quay, past the Weighbridge, so we mechanically went on loading. Some time later the captain returned and discovered that we had loaded nearer 1,500. He then ordered that the surplus be unloaded but a few minutes later realised that would be an impossible task.

So the ship sailed at once. Early in the evening the *Isle of Sark* arrived from Jersey but only people who had the usual embarkation tickets were allowed to board.

'All the evening our ticket office was besieged with people enquiring if any cancellations had been made, but none had.' said McLennan-Jones. 'Time and again people offered to pay double the usual fare but all we could do was to advise them to register to go on the evacuation boats.'

He continued:

> At 3 am Saturday morning the rush slackened and we were advised to go home but most of us just lay down on the office tables to sleep for a few hours. All day Saturday the evacuation went on, but easier now because it was all adults. I went to the Post Office but it was closed so I went into the mail entrance at the side. Only two men were on duty and they were overwhelmed with work as telegrams had been pouring in all day and they had no way of delivering them as all the messengers boys had already evacuated. I was allowed to

look through the large stack of telegrams and found one that told me the Duke of York had arrived in Weymouth. She had taken 22 hours to cross instead of the normal six.

We in the GW & SR offices had interminable arguments about whether we should stay on or leave. Four of the staff did leave but the rest of us stayed on until the last minute.

On the following Saturday (29 June) the Southern Railway steamer, the *Isle of Sark* (Captain H. H. Golding) arrived in Jersey from Southampton at 6.30 with, surprisingly, 250 passengers. Some of these could have been people who evacuated a week earlier. In her *Jersey Occupation Diary* Nan Le Ruez reports (on 24 August 1944) hearing about three evacuees who slept a night on the beach at Weymouth, went to Southampton, and then found things so bad that they returned on the last boat that came before the occupation.

When the Jersey passengers had disembarked the mailboat left for Guernsey, getting there at 12.25 p.m. with 484 passengers, almost all of whom were going to Southampton. Normally she would have sailed within an hour but it was thought prudent to travel at night so she waited in Guernsey's harbour. That evening German aircraft attacked the harbour. The crew opened fire with their four Lewis guns and a 12-pounder and the ship was not damaged except for numerous bullet marks. One passenger, a French refugee travelling to Southampton, was injured and one of the crew, Seaman Cook, received bullet wounds in the legs. Both were taken to hospital in Guernsey. The *Isle of Sark* departed at 9.54 p.m. her last voyage from the islands until after the war, arriving in Southampton at 8.30 a.m. on Saturday 29 June with 651 passengers.

Towards the end of the war Captain H.H. Golding was awarded the OBE. A news report of January 1945 reported a passenger as saying,

> When the *Isle of Sark* was bombed in Guernsey Captain Golding issued orders from the bridge and then walked along the decks keeping everyone as calm as possible. He made his presence felt wherever he went and in my judgement he was largely responsible for the steadiness of the crew, the passengers and the people on the quayside. As soon as he felt the people on board were steady he walked across the quay to telephone the naval authorities and then returned to the bridge although machine-gunning and bombing were going on at the time. When the bombing was finished he had decide how many he could take on board from the number who were clamouring on the quay.

Biddle said he made strenuous efforts in Southampton on 29 and 30 June to send steamers to the islands for more evacuees but he received a telephone message from the Bailiff of Jersey, Alexander Coutanche, which said in effect, 'No further evacuation is contemplated either from Jersey or Guernsey.'

The Bailiff told Biddle that he and the Jersey authorities would remain on the island in any circumstances. He said that more enemy planes had been over their island and it was evident that their action was directed against shipping. He believed that any attempt to send a ship to Jersey would cause the Germans to bomb the island again.

Biddle particularly remembered Coutanche's last remark to him: 'For the first time in my life I do not want to see a steamer in the harbour.'

Years later it was the memory of that channel crossing which remained firmly in the minds of many of the refugees. When the Croydon Channel Islands Society published an annual report in December 1943 it was thought fitting 'to remember with gratitude' the officers and crews of the *Viking, Antwerp, Batavia, Duke of York* and dozens of other ships that brought so many to safety. 'Crews, hollow-eyed through lack of rest, their vessels under-manned and over-loaded, with bullet and shrapnel scars and empty davits bearing testimony to many other evacuations–Dunkirk, Cherbourg and St. Malo.'

Evacuation by Air

In all that was written at the time about the evacuation emphasis was given to the sea journeys. In fact about 400 fare-paying passengers left Jersey by air on 20-21 June. Jersey Airways Ltd had continued to operate their De Havilland biplanes from the airport in the first few months of the war but in the spring of 1940 the service had to be withdrawn and the aircraft held in readiness for special British government duties.

When St Malo fell to the Germans the company made a hurried decision to transfer their Jersey office to England as soon as possible, including all the staff and their families who were willing to go. This removal was completed in their own aircraft within two days. They then turned their attention to helping with the evacuation and were given permission to use Bristol airport from where the first aircraft left in the early hours of the morning of 19 June. A few of their staff had remained in Jersey to attend to reservations and loading.

As soon as it was realised that there was a chance of getting to England by air a long queue formed at the airport. To speed up the loading (each plane had a capacity of only about 15 passengers) fares were collected on arrival. Flights were made in the daylight hours of 19-21 June but stopped after that because there was some concern about enemy attack. The pilots had reported seeing enemy aircraft and the British government refused to offer military protection because of the demilitarisation of the Channel Islands.

The Captains' Reports

The following are extracts from reports by the captains which were made to the vessels' owners later:

The **WHITSTABLE** weighed anchor in Plymouth Sound at 23.01 on 20th June and then received instructions to proceed to Jersey. After carefully threading my way through a maze of shipping in the dark, without a pilot or plan of the Sound, I finally found the break in the boom defence. On arrival off Jersey I could find no pilot, and never having been to the Channel Islands before, I had a few anxious moments threading my way through the rocks, before anchoring in St Aubins Bay at 08.22 on 21st June. At midday a pilot boarded the vessel, and at 14.35 the vessel was berthed at No. 1 berth in St Helier Harbour.

Captain Lynes of the s.s. MAIDSTONE and myself went to report to the Senior Naval Officer at the berth where he was embarking the refugees. On our way we had to pass through a large crowd of evacuees who were waiting at a barrier which was placed across the quay. Lieut. Williams, R.N.R., who was the S.N.O., informed us that both of us would embark refugees, and one of us would be the last ship to leave. He said he expected a panic and a rush on the last boat, and he suggested that we two should toss up to decide which of us would be the first to load and which would be the last to leave. This procedure being decided upon, Lynes and I made our way to the town with the object of carrying out the important business of tossing the coin in the comparative privacy of some saloon bar.

On our arrival in town we found that all the pubs were shut, and it looked as if our coin tossing would have to be done in public after all. But after trying a couple of hotel doors a complete stranger, who enquired if we were thirsty, offered to take us to a place he knew, and through his good offices we managed to obtain admittance, after a lot of bell-pushing. The door of the pub was opened just sufficient to allow us to squeeze through and when we got inside the good landlady told us the populace got a bit excited in the forenoon, and the police had advised all licensed places to close their doors. However, once we got inside we were soon outside of a nice pint of the best, and the ancient ceremony of tossing the coin was performed with due ceremony. It fell to my lot to be the first ship to embark refugees, but the S.N.O.'s programme did not work out according to plan, for when it came to my turn for embarkation there were only 70 people to ship and MAIDSTONE was sent to Guernsey. At 17.30 I berthed alongside the S.R. quay and commenced shipping five motor-cars and some government stores. Contrary to expectations, the final embarkation was both peaceful and orderly and when all were on board, including the S.N.O. himself, the vessel left at 19.42 for Weymouth.

S.S. MAIDSTONE On Thursday 20th June the MAIDSTONE was at Ocean Quay, Devonport, waiting for something to turn up, when at 2 p.m. orders were received to proceed immediately to the Channel Islands, on Admiralty account.

The ship was ready to leave at 5 p.m., but sailing was deferred until dusk, advice having been received that all lights in the islands were extinguished. The voyage was without incident, and the weather fine, and we arrived off the Corbiere at 0650 21st June.

There was no pilot on station so we continued through the Noirmont passage and anchored close to Elizabeth Castle at 07.35.

At 1300 a pilot boarded, and we proceeded into St Helier harbour and awaited our turn to load evacuees, of which there were large numbers congregated on the Weighbridge, the flow being regulated by local wardens. There appeared to be no panic, either in the town or on the quay, but it was observed that all licensed premises were closed as a precautionary measure.

SS Maidstone.

Opinion on the subject in the town was about equally divided between those who saw no immediate cause for alarm and those who could already see the Germans passing the Pierhead. There were large numbers of cars on the quay, abandoned by their owners in their haste to embark.

At 1800 hours word was received from the Sea Transport Office to proceed to Guernsey and to inform the S.T.O. there that embarkation would be finished at 1930, and to place ourselves under his orders. We arrived in Guernsey at 2100 hours and found a berth astern of the mail steamer.

Alarm at Guernsey appeared to be rather more acute than at Jersey and people were presenting themselves faster than they could be embarked, but again there was no sign of disorder.

At 0900 June 22nd we embarked 340 people, of whom about 150 were small children and the same number women. During the previous day preparations had been made to take advantage of shelter provided by alleyways (horse deck). Boards had been laid, backboards rigged, and the whole covered with clean tarpaulins and car covers. Thus, in view of the deteriorating weather, tolerably comfortable cover was provided for most.

The officers' quarters were reserved for the aged and infirm, invalids and nursing mothers. The master's cabin housed twelve infants below what might be termed fare-paying age. The feeding of these presented a problem, but they thrived on tinned milk.

We left Guernsey at 0950 in misty weather and arrived in Weymouth bay at 1600 hours, the voyage being without incident, and passengers very cheerful and making the best of uncomfortable quarters. The crew did everything possible to help and did not hesitate to forego their food in order that children might be fed. By the time we arrived in Weymouth Bay every scrap of food had gone. A day's food for twenty men did not go far between 150 hungry children.

We were sent to anchorage by the examination vessel and at 2000 hours there being so sign of any move I sent an urgent message acquainting the S.T.O. with the situation, with the result that the ship was sent alongside at 2200 hours. It was not before time, because, apart from the food situation, our 340 passengers looked like becoming 341 before many hours elapsed, and it was preferable that such an event should take place in more congenial surroundings.

S.S. DEAL made the passage to Guernsey on the night of June 20th/ 21st, arriving alongside at 0655. During the forenoon hands were employed rigging up seating accommodation in main and after holds, also in both port and starboard alleyways. A number of empty packing cases having been received from shore were used for the purpose, together with horse stall boards and seating accom-

Above: Batavier IV. *800 of the senior pupils of the Guernsey schools crossed the Channel on this Dutch cargo vessel.*
Below: SS Whitstable *was typical of the small cargo vessels used for the evacuation.*

modation for about 400 people was improvised. Both holds were swept clean and tarpaulin and truck sheets laid on the ceiling and a number of 'Capoc' life jackets were pressed into service as pillows. At about 14.15 (21st) the refugees commenced to embark. The whole of the officers and crew assisted to distribute the people comfortably about the ship. The officers and crew all very kindly gave up their quarters to as many mothers and babies as could be comfortably stowed therein. At 1606 hours (21st) we cast off and proceeded on our voyage.

The refugees evidently expected to be fed on board as none of them had brought any food with them. Again the officers and crew came to the rescue and every item of food on board was mustered up and we were able to provide tea, bread and butter, jam, etc. Two 10-gallon churns of milk were placed on board at Guernsey and this was used for feeding the babies. The vessel arrived Weymouth Roads at 22.05 (21st) and was ordered to anchor and remained at anchor until 1300 on the 22nd, when she proceeded alongside and discharged.

I would especially bring to your notice the untiring efforts of every member of the ship's company to make these mothers and babies comfortable and to help them forget their troubles. The cook remained on duty in the galley the whole 48 hours, supplying hot water and warming up milk. The seamen and firemen were distributing babies' bottles of warm milk all night and relieving tired mothers by nursing their babies for them. At 0130 on the 22nd I hailed a passing craft and requested a supply of fresh milk and bread. At 0230 a tender came alongside and put aboard 10 gallons of fresh milk, some tea, sugar, milk, jam, cheese, chocolate biscuits and margarine. The crew at once set about distributing these provisions. The number of refugees on board was 250.

S.S. HASLEMERE. On arrival in Guernsey, Thursday 20th June, I was ordered by the S.T.O. to be prepared to take evacuees to Weymouth it being intended at first that I should carry 400 adults, so holds were prepared and ladders rigged. At 1100 I was informed that I would be required to leave as soon as possible with 350 children who had been on the quay since 0300 hours. We had just pulled off fires, so it was not possible to leave until 1400 hours but we embarked the children right away to relieve pressure on the quay. We had a few women helpers with the children but by the time we were clear of the Casquets they were mostly seasick and not much use to the children, nearly all of whom were under 10 years of age.

I would like to state that everyone on board worked hard and without a break, all giving up their sleep and their beds to the children. I had four very small children in my bunk and three on the settee, and the same applies to all on board.

Evacuation Ships

The exact number of ships which took part in the evacuation was not recorded at the time but it is believed to have been at least 45. Some were Belgian and Dutch ships which had escaped from the German advance on their countries a few days earlier. The vessels included: *Antiquity, Antwerp, Archangel, Atlantic, Autocarrier, Batavier IV, Brittany, Brookfield, Caribin, Coral, Corina, Deal, Despatch, Dominion, Duke of Argyll, Duke of York, Felixstowe, Felspar, Fintain, Fratton, Glentilt, Gorecht, Haslemere, Hindsrig, Hodder, Isle of Sark, Maidstone, Malines, Nagtira, Perelle, Porthmorna, Ringwood, Saint Bedan, Seaville, Shepperton Ferry, Sheringham, Stork, Suffolk Coast, The Baron, Tonbridge, Vega, Viking, West Coaster and Whitstable.*

Most of these vessels had a gross tonnage of less than 1,000.

Chapter 3

Arrival in England

Arrivés à huit heures à Weymouth après une traversée qui avait duré neuf heures, nous débarquâmes à une heure et apprîmes que l'on avait l'intention de nous envoyer dans une ville industrielle du Lancashire. Nous étions stupéfaits. Etre obligés de quitter les plages ensoleillés et l'air limpide de Guernesey pour aller vivre dans une atmosphère de fumée, de pluie et de brouillard, voilà un avenir peu attrayant.

from an essay on the evacuation written by a pupil
at the States Intermediate School, December 1940.

It would normally be impossible for a small port such as Weymouth and small industrial towns to cope with the sudden arrival over a couple of days of thousands of homeless people. But in June 1940 the British government had already had experience of large scale evacuations and had made plans for the reception of foreign refugees.

To understand what happened to the Channel Islanders it is necessary to look briefly at events in Britain of a few months earlier.

As early as 1934 an evacuation sub-committee had reported secretly to the government and by the time war was declared on 3 September 1939 plans were already in operation for a large-scale evacuation of children from cities.

In a few days almost one and a half million people, mostly children but including the blind, the homeless and about 100,000 mothers, from London, Birmingham, Manchester, Newcastle and other cities had been put on trains which took them to the countryside where they were billeted. Some MPs had asked the Government to consider building large camps but in view of the enormous number of evacuees, home billeting was thought to be the only suitable answer.

All sorts of difficulties soon became apparent. Trains packed with hungry children, and sometimes without lavatories, were delayed, there was often confusion about destinations and at the end of the journey there was much resentment at the way children were paraded in village halls, or made to walk in

Opposite: Weymouth Harbour in 1940. Over 23,000 CI refugees disembarked here between 20-25 June.

35

groups along streets lined with terraced houses whilst householders picked the ones they preferred.

The experience gained with this evacuation of September, 1939 enabled staff at the Ministry and in local authorities to iron out some of the problems which arose when large numbers of evacuees were moved. Furthermore arrangements had also been made for the reception of foreign refugees from the continent. On 12 April certain local authorities were sent a long, confidential circular advising them what action they should take 'to meet the possibility of an influx of refugees from Holland and Belgium in the event of an attack by Germany on those countries. The Government will...accept responsibility for any additional cost incurred by local authorities in feeding these refugees and providing them with temporary shelter.' It was assumed 'that the amount of shipping in the ports of Holland and Belgium will permit the escape directly by sea of at the most 100,000 refugees...Temporary accommodation on land will be found in the neutral areas of Lancashire, Cheshire and the West Riding for refugees landed at the Mersey...'

A letter dated 10 May 1940 from the Minister of Health, Walter Elliot, asked the councils of towns in these areas to help with the reception of evacuees from the continent. It ended, 'I need not dwell on the claims that these refugees have on our help. They are now our Allies and I am sure that I can rely on your co-operation and that of your district in this war work.'

As a result of the 1939 evacuation and the preparations for refugees from the continent, the movement of large numbers of homeless Channel Islanders to the reception areas in the north was, although not without hitches, far more expeditious than it would otherwise have been.

By the time Paris fell in the middle of June few refugees from the Continent had arrived in the UK but a number of Dutch ships had escaped to England when Holland was occupied. For these reasons the British government had been able to send a number of foreign vessels to the Channel Islands and was now able to make use of the arrangements which had recently been planned in the northern towns.

The arrival in Weymouth

The Ministry instructions to local authorities were that 'one or more large halls, covered markets or similar places should be requisitioned if necessary.'

In Weymouth the borough council (Weymouth & Melcombe Regis) had taken over the Pavilion Theatre, a wooden building built in 1908. (After the war the Pavilion was renamed The Ritz. It was destroyed by fire in 1954. A new theatre opened on the site in 1960).

The Ministry had asked that 'Some medical inspection as time permits should be done in the course of landing and in the assembly hall before the distribution to trains.' To help with this when the Channel Islanders arrived the Ministry sent a medical officer from London but, in the words of the Circular. 'It will probably not be practicable to make any close inspection for infectious disease.'

Above: The Pavilion Theatre at Weymouth Harbour. Many of the refugees rested in here on arrival. The building was destroyed by fire in 1954.
Below: CI refugees arriving in Weymouth.

A report by St John Ambulance gives the total number of CI evacuees who arrived in Weymouth from 20-28 June as 23,743. The private diary of the GWR Traffic and marine agent, D.G. Hoppins, mentions that 'between 20 June and 28 June, 25,484 evacuees were landed at Weymouth from 55 ships, 20 from Jersey, 30 from Guernsey and 5 from Alderney.'

According to the St John Ambulance report all arrivals were labelled. A large majority, 23,213, were "N.A.D." (Nothing Abnormal Detected). 96 were MAT (Maternity) and a small number were either SS (Surgical Sick) or MS (Medical Sick).

In fact the medical inspections, according to the evacuees who have reported on this, consisted of no more than a brief glance and a question as to whether they were well.

The simple formalities in Weymouth were prolonged because of the small number of officials, medical and immigration, who were present. Buses were used to carry evacuees the short distance to the railway station but the special trains arrived at irregular intervals and there were long waits. Many people must have felt so disoriented that they failed to put their luggage on the train. Two weeks later, on 4 July, the Ministry of Health wrote to the local authorities in the reception areas to say that 'a considerable amount of luggage was left behind by the evacuees at Weymouth.' This led to a lot of correspondence between council officials and evacuees in the months that followed. Lists describing separate items were posted up in the reception areas.

One of the St. John Ambulance men, D.G.F. Acutt, who attended the arrivals in Weymouth said in his memoirs published in 1946 that an 'enormous number of baskets of tomatoes' were brought by the evacuees. 'Many a basket,' he added, 'found its way into a Weymouth home during the evacuation...for the islanders were most generous in their distribution of them.' Mr Acutt also mentions that the voluntary helpers were astonished to see the arrival of so many children, accompanied only by their teachers.

Most of the evacuees' trains left during the late afternoon or evening. For some the long night journey to the north in the crowded compartments (the coaches of most trains in those days were divided into compartments designed for six or eight passengers) was just as unpleasant as the sea journey. None had any idea where they were going or how long the journey would take. Although most ended the journey in either Lancashire or Yorkshire, some went on as far as Glasgow.

A number of children became separated from their parents or from their school parties at Weymouth, or on the rail journeys, and were not reunited for several days or weeks.

The Weymouth daily newspaper, the *Dorset Daily Echo*, was at first silent on the evacuation. A small item on the front page of 22 June merely reporting under the headline REFUGEES ARE POURING INTO BRITAIN that 'several thousand French, Belgian & British have reached a west country port in the past two or three days.'

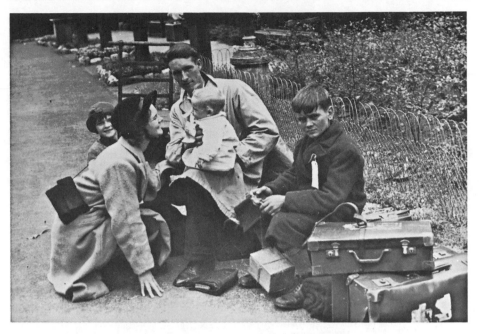

Labelled in Weymouth. This family is waiting in a park to be taken to the railway station.

Although the evacuation was not reported air raids on Jersey and Guernsey were the main front page headline on 29 June. An inside story on the same day gave the impression that the islands had all been completely evacuated, reporting:

HOW CHANNEL ISLANDERS
PUT THE SHUTTERS UP
90,000 CROSSED TO MAINLAND

After the garrisons were withdrawn began the evacuation of 90,000 men, women and children. Next to Dunkirk it is an epic story of the war. The children were got away first. It was a story of good discipline, perfect organisation and fine courage. Many came to a south coast port which in happier times had sent over summer holiday invaders in their tens of thousands. First to come were the youngest tots. With dolls in their arms and their possessions in pathetic bundles they came off the boats singing and cheering.

A schoolmaster said, "We were packed liked herrings, seven or eight hundred of us. The children had behaved like true Britishers and so had their parents who were left behind. I had pleaded with the mothers and fathers to face up to the situation with courage.

They kissed their children in affectionate farewell. I locked my schoolhouse and said good-bye to my home, I don't suppose I shall ever see it again.'

One of Jersey's biggest poultry farmers said, 'The last thing I did was to throw all the corn to the chicken, thousands of them, and leave them to it.'

The reception arrangements at a port of disembarkation worked with smooth efficiency. WVS workers, ministers of religion, and many others worked in day and night shifts in public gardens near the pier to supply refreshments to the refugees before they left in special trains to their new homes. It was a triumph of organisation and an historic example of English hospitality for homeless ones from these islands of life, love and laughter and care-free holiday gaiety.

The rail journey from Weymouth was an exciting adventure for many of the boys, many of whom had never seen a train before.

Arrival in the North

Early in 1940 the Ministry of Health had asked local authorities in Lancashire, Cheshire and the West Riding of Yorkshire to estimate how much temporary accommodation they could provide for refugees. Replies had varied widely from a few hundred to over one thousand. It was this information that enabled the Ministry to direct the trains filled with Channel Islanders to Barnsley, Bradford, Brighouse, Burnley, Bury, Doncaster, Glasgow, Halifax, Huddersfield, Leeds, Nantwich, Oldham, Rochdale, St Helens, Stockport, Wakefield, and other towns.

Looking back at the local newspaper reports in these areas the event seems to have been a welcome break of considerable interest in the life of the community. There was no shortage of volunteers to give whatever help was needed. One newspaper, describing the enthusiastic welcome, said that although the police had asked for 30 special constables to meet a train at four in the morning, 73 had paraded. Many of the reports covered the arrivals at length and some included photographs with prominent headlines. Readers were not told, however, exactly where the strangers had come from but a perceptive reader could easily identify their origin. They were British, they had unusual foreign-looking names like Pallot, and Gallienne, and some of the children were reported to have said they'd never before seen a train or black cows.

Here for example is the headline from the *Stockport Advertiser* of 28 June:

1,200 EVACUEES ARRIVE IN STOCKPORT
Billeted in Public Buildings

Last Saturday and Sunday two stages in one of the most remarkable episodes in the history of the Borough of Stockport were enacted when about 1,200 evacuees from a dangerous area arrived in the town.

School children, with their teachers and helpers, had arrived at 4.45 on Saturday morning. Despite the early hour they were welcomed by the Mayor (Alderman T.E. Hunt, JP) and Mrs Hunt, members of the A.R.P. Emergency Committee, the Town Clerk (Mr Frank Knowles) and other chief officials of the town, with a number of voluntary workers. A fleet of cars took the children to various reception centres which included the Town Hall, the Masonic Guildhall, the Reform Club, the Savoy Dance Hall and several schools.

The report was long but the journalist evidently felt much more could have been said for he added, 'Such in outline is a story, which if told in detail, would rank amongst the epics of Stockport, but in war-time a good deal of reticence is necessary even at the risk of spoiling an absorbing tale of adventure.'

It was accompanied by a photograph of smiling children at the entrance to the Town Hall and showing, according to the caption, 'toys and books sent for them by local inhabitants.'

The number and variety of these so impressed one of the Guernsey teachers, P. J. Martel, that he wrote later:

> They [toys and books] came pouring into the rest centre by the armful, by the basketful, and even by the car load. True, a family of 200 children takes some amusing, but the motor cars, speed boats, trains, acrobats, puzzles, dolls' houses, dolls, Teddy bears, rocking horses, etc. left the children speechless, with just glaring eyes. A kind gentleman brought five car loads. 'I've collected these from friends,' he said, 'I've got plenty more.'

The *Stockport Express* (27 June 1940) carried a similar report under the headline WAR VICTIMS IN STOCKPORT:

> Folk told how they had left all their possessions behind them, of a 24-hour wait for a boat with the constant threat of bombing raids, of a zig-zag course on a very crowded steamer manned by Poles and Norwegians, and a wait outside the harbour before they landed at a British port.

By July, although many had not yet been billeted or had not found satisfactory accommodation, the islanders were feeling more confident about the future and were grateful to their hosts for the warm and sympathetic welcome they had received. Typical of letters received by local newspapers at the time was this one from the Guernseyman, A. Sandford Blicq, who had been editor of the *Evening Press* and at the time he wrote was still living in temporary accommodation at Horse Carrs, Rochdale. He said he wanted

> ...to convey to the warm-hearted and generous people of Rochdale how greatly everyone from Guernsey appreciates the typical Lancashire kindness that has been showered upon us. The wonderful kindness of the people of Rochdale has done very much more than a letter can convey to lighten the burden of the many who have lost their homes and possessions...I must emphasise how much the children have benefited from Rochdale's welcome. These children have come from the sunshine and golden sands and open spaces of an island home to the hustle of an intensely industrialised centre. The cold change in environment could easily have overwhelmed them. The great-hearted sympathy and the charm of the people of Rochdale has made all the difference.

In Yorkshire on the same day the *Halifax Daily Courier* reported that 400 Channel Island evacuees had arrived at 5 a.m. in Halifax and 151 in Brighouse.

> They had been travelling for two days and two nights and were in a pitiable plight owing to lack of sleep and the suddenness of their evacuation. Many of the woman had babies and young children. Some of them, clinging to a few household goods, presented a pathetic picture. One elderly woman, able to move about only in a bath chair, had borne the trying journey with fortitude. A large proportion of the people had never been away from the Channel Islands. Though mostly bi-lingual they speak English. British subjects, they are homely, frugal, hard-working people.

Yvonne Russell a girl of 20 travelling with her father remembers her arrival in Halifax:

> It was dark and it looked very bleak. It had a funny smell which turned out to be smoke from factory chimneys. It was horrible. We were put into buses. I remember being told I would be separated from my father, but we managed to stick together. Our destination was a large, stark building. We were all hungry and thirsty. We were given a meal of soup and bread and tin mugs of tea. After our meal we were shown to a large room where there were piles of mattresses and blankets ready for us. Lots of English people were there with spare clothes. They couldn't have been kinder.

In the morning Yvonne discovered that she was in the Halifax Workhouse. It was surrounded by high railings and a large gate was locked with padlocks. They were kept there for three days. 'People were great to us,' she wrote later. 'We tried to get news of my mother and brothers but no-one knew anything.'

In many other towns in the north of England and in Scotland similar sentiments were being expressed. It would be impossible in the space available here to cover events in each town. Bury in Lancashire was typical in the way the local officials and the people generally accepted the burden of the sudden influx of thousands of strangers.

Bury

Bury in 1940 was a town with a population of 60,000. In number this was close to Jersey's pre-war population but the County Borough of Bury was very different in atmosphere and appearance from St Helier. The busy shopping streets were spacious enough for trams. Beyond the shopping centre were long streets of terraced houses, cotton mills, paper works and factories of which major products were slippers, confectionery and furniture. Tall chimneys were a conspicuous feature but beyond the smoky haze of the town you could see hills rising to the moors which surround the town. Bury was considered fortunate in having a diversity of industry so that it did not rely so much on cotton as some of the other northern towns.

Like many similar towns in the north, Bury received confidential instructions in April 1940 from the Ministry of Health that the town must expect to receive refugees at short notice The Town Clerk was told that he should not disclose to any member of the council other than the Chairman the contents of the Ministry letters. 'There is no evidence that such an emergency is imminent,' said the Ministry. If urgent action becomes necessary you will receive a telegram *Prepare for War Refugees*. The Clerk secretly agreed with the Mayor that fifty new houses being built as part of a slum clearance scheme would be reserved for such an emergency.

The warning telegram arrived on 10 May and a letter saying that the Ministry estimated they would be allocated 500 refugees. The news was immediately released to the town that refugees were expected.

'The majority shall be accommodated for the duration of the war in suitable empty houses and some may be received into private households,' said the press release, and then spelled out the payment that would be made to householders for billeting: 'One guinea a week for each single adult, 35/- for husband and wife, 10/6d for a child 14-17 and 8/6d for a child under 14.'

The public image of local government, or the 'Town hall bureaucracy' is frequently not a happy one. Officials are often accused of unnecessary delays and formalities. But here in Bury, as with many other towns to which refugees were sent by central government, senior officials and leading members of the council, acted with commendable speed, conscientiously following the voluminous instructions from Whitehall and utilising local voluntary help in a most effective way.

By the time the Channel Islanders arrived at the end of June many people had been involved in the preparations for their reception. The *Bury Times* reported that on the night of Friday, 21 June:

> While most of Bury slept a small army of workers made up for the most part of members of the WVS, school teachers, first aid parties, the Emergency Relief organisation of the Civil Defence scheme, special constables, town council officials and their staffs and a host of others, but despite the urgency of the arrangements this well-ordered and excellently ordered evacuation was carried through without any great discomfort to any of the visitors.

Later in the week there were similar articles and photographs, often emphasising that the refugees were not foreigners and pointing out that the children in the photographs were 'fair-haired youngsters.'

Above: The Chesham Fold housing estate in Bury. Fifty of these houses were allocated to CI refugees.
Below: With its numerous factory chimneys, Bury seemed a depressing place to the refugees.

BRITISH EVACUEES FIND HOMES IN BURY

They had travelled many hundreds of miles without a break of any kind, They came in a long thin line from Knowsley Street Station after a 14-hour journey. Mothers had babies to push in prams as well as to carry their own bundles. Men carried their belongings in cases and parcels; one had blankets strapped to his back. Their welcome centre was the Palais-de-Danse. It must have been a pleasant change for them to turn into the well lit dance hall with sandwiches and cakes and hot tea and coffee waiting and bright music to cheer them and dispel, momentarily at least, the pangs some of those smaller children must have felt in leaving behind their homes and their parents.   (*Bury Times*, 26 June 1940)

When Bury had first been told to expect refugees it was expected that they would be in families. The fact a large proportion of the Channel Islanders were children in large groups had, in the words of the Town Clerk, 'made it extremely difficult.'

From an orphanage in Guernsey, had arrived without warning 51 children of school age and 11 babies, with some of the staff. Bury was able to accommodate these in an old workhouse building, Danesmoor, where Mr Harry Brown who been manager of the orphanage in Guernsey, continued to be in charge for the remainder of the war. As the children in his care reached the age of 14 he was able to place them in employment such as domestic service, and as farm labourers. He was also able to receive unwanted children born to Channel Islands refugees during the war.

The children of Guernsey's Castel School numbering 74 girls and 78 boys with twelve teachers and the wives of two teachers also arrived in Bury. These were in addition to several groups of children from other schools travelling with their teachers, or children who had become separated from their school groups and were virtually lost. In the days following their arrival the staff of the Town Clerk's department were put to some trouble sorting out these children, locating the appropriate school party in another town, and despatching them to join the right teachers.

The Town Hall received numerous letters asking if there was any record of a particular child. One teacher wrote a postcard to Bury saying that he had lost four boys and one girl.

Most of these letters of enquiry received a short printed reply, 'I have to inform you that there are no children in Bury of that name.' A few parents, some as far away as London or Glasgow, received a positive reply from the Clerk, 'I have to inform you that (name) is staying at (address).'

One parent, on hearing that her son David was in Bury, wrote from Devizes in Wiltshire on 26 July 1940, 'I am sorry to say that my husband and I are not in a financial position to fetch David. My husband has not got a constant job and my daughter is being sent from Glasgow.'

David was sent to Devizes with an adult evacuee as escort on 9 August. His mother wrote on 13 August to the Town Clerk of Bury, "...to thank you for what you done for him, he says he was very happy at the hospital [the Jericho Institution, an old workhouse]. Would you ask the lady he was billeted with to send his clothes, ration book and gas mask."

On the morning Sunday 7 July the Clerk arranged for buses to take 221 children and their teachers to Bucklow, Cheshire.

By this time, the names of the refugees' homeland could no longer be kept a secret. The *Bury Times*, reflecting the considerable public interest in the Channel Islanders, reported this move at length, with photographs:

> They came as they had come. Their worldly belongings were slung in brown paper parcels and little valises over their backs as they had been 14 days before when they arrived in Bury, a travel-tired and weary company. But anybody who saw their parting on Sunday morning and there were many dozens of townsfolk standing at street corners waving to them, must have seen a difference. There were tears of course for these little Guernsey folk have learned in a fortnight the real value of the generosity the Lancastrian can extend to any who come face to face with dire adversity. Exemplary care has been taken to make them happy.

Meanwhile arrangements were being made at the Town Hall to receive replacement Channel Islanders who were homeless. 'There are many families in Bolton for whom accommodation is required,' the Town Clerk was reported to have said, 'and we feel the least we can do is to offer them the empty houses on the Chesham Estate.'

It was to be many weeks before the refugees, whether they were children with their teachers, or whole families, were able to settle into their new lives. In the next chapter we shall look at what happened to one large family who made a sudden decision to evacuate, leaving their home and most of their possessions in Jersey.

HOME

Three years is such a long, long time,
To leave the ones we loved behind.
We pray. We hope. They understand
How we all fare in this strange land.
There isn't much that we can say,
Although we would all gladly pay
The price, no matter what it cost
To speak, just once to those we've lost.
But courage, Sarnians, wear that smile;
We've roughed the worst, it's been worth while.
We've turned the tide, it won't be long,
Our spirits right, our hearts still strong.
Remember, as the boat makes fast,
It's Home. Our Home, we're there at last.

Doris Le Parmentier
July 1943

HOLD ON

Comrades in exile, be brave of heart,
Though pining for those you hold dear.
Pluck up your courage with thoughts of return
And hopes that reunion is near.
The view from Bonne Nuit will still be the same,
For nothing can change the blue sea.
Your favourite haunt will welcome you still
Though altered perhaps it may be.
You can still fish from St Catherine's wall,
That breakwater worn and grey.
Mont Orgueil castle will still look down
As it did on our parting day.
The Vinchelez lanes will retain their cool shade,
The sunshine will sparkle as bright.
The island with joy will be welcomed again
When Corbiere comes once more in sight.

Sheila Le Boutillier, aged 12.
November 1943

Chapter 4

Experiences of the Cox family

---

*If our boat should not reach England and any of the children are saved, I
know you will always do your best for them. Just now it is such a relief to
know I can depend on you.*

Mrs A.G. Cox on 19 June 1940 in a letter
to her eldest daughter in London

Somehow, despite the trauma caused by the sudden decision to abandon her
home at 24 hours' notice, packing minimum requirements for her family, and
destroying personal papers and mementoes Mrs Cox found time to pause at
midnight and write a long letter recording the events of the day.

In 1921, Leonard Cox, a sergeant in the Royal Corps of Military Accountants,
had been posted to Jersey. By 1940 he was a bookkeeper at Noel & Porter, the big
department store in King Street, St Helier. He and his wife Alyce rented a
spacious town house, 11 Duhamel Place, which they ran as a boarding house.
They had six children. In June 1940 Bryan was 21, Audrey 19, Graeme 17, Ronald
15, Beryl 12, and Sheila 8 years old.

Life had not been easy for the Cox family. Wages were low in the 1930s and
with such a large family there was little money to spare for luxuries such as
holidays outside Jersey.

By the beginning of 1940 family prospects would have been brighter but for
the war. The three eldest children had left school. Bryan was employed by the
Jersey New Water Works Company and was studying for a degree in civil
engineering, Audrey had gone to London and was working with H.M. Customs
& Excise and Graeme was a clerk in the office of the local bus company (JMT).

Because of the war few holidaymakers were coming to the islands and by June
1940 Mrs Cox had not taken any booking at all for the year.

The War gets nearer

Graeme had built himself a short wave radio receiver. He recalls that during 1940
he used to listen to the German propaganda broadcasts by Lord Haw-Haw. 'Not
for information,' he says, 'but for fun. They were very amusing.'

He remembers hearing Lord Haw Haw saying in early 1940 that he would soon be coming to the Channel Islands. At the time Graeme and his family thought this incredible. It was impossible to imagine a foreign power taking over. Even with the Germans breaking through the Maginot line in eastern France they and most Channel Islanders found it inconceivable that Jersey would be seriously affected by the war.

But on Sunday 9th June 1940 Jersey began to see war on the southern horizon. Black smoke was rising from the French coast as the French burnt oil storage tanks to prevent the fuel getting into the hands of the enemy. In her letter of 19 June Mrs Cox wrote, 'Yesterday the gunfire could be heard quite distinctly. Two ships were shelling the coat at Avranches. St Malo is finished and the harbour destroyed by our troops before leaving.'

The Militia goes

The eldest son in the family, Bryan, was an enthusiastic member of Jersey's Royal Militia (RMIJ) which he had joined on leaving Victoria College OTC. Until 1928 military service for the Island's young men had been compulsory but since that year the British government had refused to contribute to the cost so service had been voluntary. The Battalion had been mobilised at the outbreak of war in 1939 and since then had been providing guards at various points in the Island such as the airport and the harbour.

When the orders were received on the night of the 18th/19th June that the islands were to be demilitarised the commanding officer paraded the Battalion to explain the position. He said that he was going to England to fight, and that a ship was available (a potato vessel, the SS Hodder). Those who were willing to go with him should take one pace forward. 'The whole Battalion then advanced one pace...so that was that!' wrote Colonel Vatcher, MC, after the war.

Sergeant Bryan Cox was the Guard Commander on Fort Regent at the time. He remembers what he describes as 'a hectic night' as all military stores were made ready for loading on the Hodder.

They knew they would be going north but like most of the evacuees had no idea where. When the master of the Hodder asked Colonel Vatcher where he was to go, the Colonel asked for suggestions.

'I have the course to Weymouth and to Southampton,' replied the ship's Captain. The colonel chose Southampton and they sailed at three in the afternoon of June 20th with 204 uniformed men, including eleven officers, as well as a number of civilian evacuees. The ship dropped anchor in Southampton Water at nine on the following morning but when the great number of weapons such as rifles, machine guns, etc. was seen it was detained for several hours, suspected of being an invading force because news of the evacuation had not been released.

Leaving home

When the news of the evacuation broke on the 19th the younger children were playing on the beach at West Park, about 3⁄4 mile from their home, because it was such a fine day. Mrs Cox heard the news from a neighbour. She recorded later that day that she was '…so upset, went to West Park to call the family. The guns at West Park had gone, and the anti-aircraft ones were only placed there this morning. Armoured lorries, loaded, were rushing to the pier, so I knew it was true. Crowds everywhere discussing the news, many wet-eyed.'

That evening, 'Daddy and I went to the Town Hall at 7.15 and took our place opposite the Cenotaph in the queue, which was six abreast.' At 10 p.m., when they had nearly reached the Town Hall and the queue stretched into Gloucester Street (1/4 mile) the office closed and they were told to come back at 5 a.m. Mr Cox returned at that time and eventually registered the family for evacuation.

Graeme remembers that his father came home from the shop on the 19th with his week's wages of £2.10/-. On the 20th they took all their coal from the coal-shed and gave it to one of the neighbours. 'We also gave away two of the family's prized possessions, an Electrolux vacuum cleaner which was kept in a beauti-fully polished wooden box, and a Singer sewing machine.' Mrs Cox also sent some treasured books, including Bryan's leather-bound College prizes, to the public library. 'I hated to think of those left for anybody,' she wrote.

Graeme also recalls that his mother and father stayed up all night sorting out their possessions and trying to decide what they could take in their luggage allowance of 28 lbs each. All their correspondence and papers going back to 1918 were burnt in the wash-house copper on the following morning. They buried a .22 rifle and an antique sword in the yard. By midday on Friday they had packed their bags. 'We only had one reasonably sized suitcase and four small ones,' Mrs Cox wrote later. In addition to clothing they had packed a few sheets, table-cloths and some silver-plated cutlery. They carried sandwiches in a wicker shopping basket. Graeme took the key of the house to the landlady in New Street and paid her the £2 rent for the last week. The neighbour to whom they had given many of their possessions gave them a lift in his car to the quayside.

They waited in the large crowd, directed first to the Weymouth pier, and later to the Albert Pier. As different vessels came into the harbour the crowds surged forward, trying to position themselves to get on board a ship. A few policemen controlled the crowds at barriers, allowing fifty through at a time.

Beryl recalls that at one stage it seemed that father would be left behind. As her two brothers went aboard a coal-boat the vessel was declared full. After an unsuccessful attempt to board another ship, the family returned to the boys' coal-boat. "Will you please just take my wife and daughters?" said Mr Cox. "I'm not going. I'm too old."

The man on the gangway agreed. Then, as he saw the tearful farewells, he said, "Oh, come on, old man, get on!"

The ship was the *Porthmorna*, a cargo vessel of 1,000 tons built in 1910. The family settled down on the hatch cover of a hold. They had each brought a blanket. 'Ugh! The weight of those cumbersome things!' wrote Mrs Cox later. 'But very glad we did, or we should have frozen.'

'What a glorious evening,' Mrs Cox continued. 'I shall never forget it. The sea perfect, the sun shining on a high tide.' Later they saw the setting sun, and the full moon rising. 'We thought it wonderful especially since others have told us of their trials. Some were in the coal-hold of one boat and everybody was sick all night with one bucket between them.'

The sea crossing was uncomfortable but uneventful. It was the first time the children had been to England. Beryl remembered being quite frightened on the journey but, she said, her brothers were very excited and impatient to get ashore.

At about 4 a.m. it began to get light. Graeme saw a paddle steamer coming alongside with a pilot. Not long after that there was land ahead. "The silence and gloom lifted at once," says Graeme, "People began to sing 'There'll always be an England' 'Rule Britannia' and 'The White Cliffs of Dover.'"

The ship berthed in Weymouth at 9 a.m. They had eaten half the sandwiches the previous evening and now as they picked up their bags to disembark they looked for the basket, but it was gone. They could only assume that it had been stolen. They were so hungry that the loss of those sandwiches seemed the most important thing in the world at that moment, said Graeme later.

They walked in a long line with other evacuees to the nearby Pavilion Theatre in Weymouth. Here there was much queuing. Mrs Cox remembered, 'great crowds, several people fainting. We waited two or three hours for a brief medical examination and then were questioned by security officers.'

Later they were allowed to sit in the theatre seats and were given cups of tea, sandwiches and biscuits. 'That tea was like heaven,' Mrs Cox wrote a few days later.

The ladies serving these refreshments were the members of the Women's Voluntary Services (WVS), a new organisation which had been set up in 1938 to arrange voluntary service in time of need. As will be seen later the Channel Islands refugees were to receive a vast amount of help in different ways from the WVS members in different parts of the country.

After the formalities on arrival in Weymouth the refugees were asked if they had relatives or friends who could accommodate them in the UK. If so, they were free to make their own way and were offered free railways warrants if they had no money to pay for the journey. A large majority, including the Cox family, had nowhere to go and very little money. These were now given identification labels to pin on their clothing. After further waiting they were eventually taken on buses to Weymouth station.

'We got to the station at 4.30 in the afternoon,' Mrs Cox wrote later. 'Then we had to sit on our luggage. But nobody could do enough for us. The YMCA had a buffet, and we were given tea, cheese sandwiches, and biscuits – all free.'

Rumours abounded and the evacuees were not given any official information. This secrecy is said by some historians to have been a deliberate policy at the time which stemmed from an idea at government level that all large movements of people might be subject to enemy sabotage. It is more likely to have been the result of an oversight when plans for receiving large numbers of refugees were made at Whitehall as well as a desire to move people to safe areas at minimum cost. Mrs Cox remembered that one of the rumours was that they would be taken to a camp four miles outside Weymouth.

Eventually a long empty train came in. 'We were lucky,' wrote Mrs Cox. 'We managed to get a compartment for the six of us.' Some families were broken up and in some cases there were as many as ten to a compartment designed for six.

The Cox family in 1940. Left to right: Sheila, Alyce, Graeme, Beryl, Ronald, Audrey, Bryan, Leonard.

The train journey

As the train pulled out of Weymouth the passengers had no idea that they would be travelling all night. For the children it was a great adventure. Most had never seen a train before, let alone travelled on one. Nor had they ever seen a bridge or a river, or sheep. But what many remembered most strongly and mentioned in their essays and comments later, were 'black cows.' (Channel Island cattle are almost all pale fawn in colour).

It was evident that the public was aware that these long and crowded trains moving north were packed with refugees.

Hamel, in his book *X-Iles* recalls that when they stopped at one station a railwayman called out, "You'll be OK here, the spirit of the people in England is on top!" He also remembered groups of people in towns and villages standing and watching the train as it passed by. At one point the train stopped just outside Bristol near a row of houses and 'from these houses came a stream of children.' carrying bottles of lemonade which they handed up to the people on the train.

For Graeme Cox the memory of this stop has remained with him all his life. 'The engine driver sounded his whistle several times and hundreds of people suddenly appeared on the embankment carrying biscuits, jugs of drink and sandwiches. Apparently they were accustomed to providing refreshments for troops and evacuees. We could not find enough words to thank these people for their generosity and kindness.'

Mrs Cox, in her letter written two days later, also remarks on this stop. It was 'on a cutting, where two roads met, a poor quarter. We threw coppers and Jersey pennies,' she wrote. ' A policemen tried to turn them off but they still came. Boys said they keep things in readiness for the troop trains which stop here.'

During the week of the evacuation a number of fully-laden trains travelled north. These went mainly to counties which had been designated by the British government as 'neutral areas' – Lancashire , Cheshire and the West Riding of Yorkshire. Because of the heavy demand some of the rolling stock was unsuitable for long journeys. A few coaches were non-corridor, normally used only for local journeys. Yvonne Russell, a Guernsey girl of 15 at the time of the evacuation has recorded in her reminiscences the embarrassment felt by the ten people of mixed ages and sexes who were packed in a compartment in a non-corridor coach which for hours did not stop long enough for people to get out and relieve themselves.

As the train on which the Cox family travelled headed north it passed within a mile and a half of Wotton-under-Edge where Mr Cox was born. Beryl remembers her interest as her father pointed out places he had known in his youth. Throughout the night they dozed fitfully. As dawn broke '…it was raining and we were passing through horrible country,' wrote Mrs Cox.

The spirits of the people on the train were low. They were hungry, tired and depressed by the unfolding landscape which seemed so dark and dreary.

Arrival in Rochdale

The evacuees did not know that municipal authorities had been warned to expect a large number of refugees.

No-one on the train in which the Cox family travelled would have been aware at the time that it was expected to arrive in Lancashire in the early hours of the morning. The Town Clerk of Rochdale (Mr H. Bann), with the Public Assistance officer (Mr J. Wilson) and Lady Turner, with other members of the WVS, were waiting on Rochdale station at 1.30 a.m. but the train didn't arrive until 5.30 a.m.

Graeme remembers that as the train pulled into the station he was able to reading a painted-out sign ROCHDALE. He, like most of those on the train, had never heard of the place. Then someone mentioned that it was where Gracie Fields came from.

"This trivial bit of information was strangely comforting," Graeme said later. "I'd seen Gracie Fields in films and I felt that if they were like her in Rochdale we would be all right!"

Corporation buses were waiting outside the station. 670 evacuees were taken to three large empty houses on the outskirts of Rochdale which had been specially prepared by the WVS for evacuees, but not necessarily English speaking people. These houses were Westfield, Horse Carrs and Roylelands. Rochdale had been told to expect a large influx of Belgian and Dutch people but in fact these never materialised and the Channel Island people had the benefit of arrangements that had been made for others.

The *Rochdale Observer* reported in the following week:

> The three houses have been a source of many hours work for the WVS for the last three months. They have been thoroughly cleaned, second-hand clothes have been prepared, crockery and cutlery collected. The WVS members provided hot soup, tea, sandwiches and hot water.

Horse Carrs, Rochdale, one of the reception centres.

Women and girls were in some rooms, men and boys in others. 'There are 16 beds in our room, camp beds, no spare inch.' wrote Mrs Cox in a letter (headed

Westfield Evacuation Centre) to Audrey the next day, a Sunday. 'Everyone is so kind. We are pressed to eat. Our supper is tea or coffee, bread and butter and cake. Two lady doctors have been to see all the children. This morning we were escorted to church as we are not really allowed out until we have registered.' The beds were simple folding camp beds and as covers they were given lengths of tweed from the local mills.

Graeme remembered their reception as 'basic but very wonderful because the people of Rochdale were so welcoming.' They registered at the Town Hall the next day and 'We were given passes to take to the old-fashioned public baths where we could have free baths.'

The refugees were encouraged to help with the running of the house and Mr Cox was put in charge of the group, a responsibility he welcomed.

In London on Thursday 20 June, a telephone call from a friend who had just arrived from Jersey alerted Audrey to the evacuation. On Friday she learnt by telegram that the family had reached Weymouth. On Saturday her mother's epic letter arrived. Finally, on Sunday, a telegram brought the news that they were in Rochdale. At about the same time she heard that Bryan had crossed safely with the militia.

Audrey has never forgotten the impact of her first visit to Rochdale with its tall chimneys smoking day and night, the dank atmosphere even when the sun shone, the clatter of clogs on the cobbled streets and the all-pervading smell of the gas works. It was a world of complete contrast to the island the refugees had left. But time would prove that any apprehension or depression arising from their plunge into this disconcerting environment would be greatly mitigated by the warm welcome, compassion and kindness of Rochdale's inhabitants who rallied in force to help them.

Life in Lancashire

Rochdale was one of the small towns around Manchester that developed rapidly in the nineteenth century as an important textile centre, producing mainly cotton goods and, to a lesser extent, wool. Cotton mills were a part of the town's landscape and there were many tall chimneys typical of the industrial north. There was considerable pollution by coal smoke, not only from industry but from the domestic chimneys of many streets of red-brick terraced houses.

We can only guess now at the feelings that many of the Channel Island people must have had about their futures. They heard soon after they arrived that their islands had been bombed and then occupied by enemy forces but they had no other news. What sort of horrors would now be taking place at home? What was their future here without jobs, homes or money in this bleak industrial area?

The six members of the Cox family settled down well at Westfield, fortified perhaps by the unity of the family. They had no relatives in Jersey whereas many of the other refugees were lone women with children or couples who had left close relatives in their island homes.

Graeme and his father, who was then a greying man of 59, began to take long walks about the town. They were surprised to find that there were many houses available to rent. Eventually they took a fancy to No. 17 St Albans' Street, the end of a terrace facing a park and not far from the town centre. The house had been empty for some time and the landlord was glad to find someone to occupy it.

They had no furniture but to their astonishment, as soon as it became known to the neighbours that they were about to move in, they were given all sorts of household items, including furniture, crockery, cutlery, saucepans, etc. This was the experience of many of the other Channel Islanders who moved into rented houses at the time. This generosity was partly a result of advertisements appealing for spare items of furniture which had been placed in the local newspaper by the Public Assistance Officer, Mr. J. Wilson.

Mr Cox was soon able to get a job. He became a local agent for the Prudential Insurance Company. On 24 July Ronald was appointed as a junior clerk in the Ensor Mill office at March Barn, Rochdale. Soon after this he enrolled in the Air Training Corps. When the Rochdale & District CI Society was formed in 1941 he took an active part, becoming treasurer in 1943 until he joined the Royal Air Force.

Graeme was offered a job as an office worker at a sand and gravel quarry at 15/- a week, the same as he had been getting in Jersey. He recalls that one of his duties was to answer the telephone but he often had difficulty in understanding the northern accents. He wasn't happy in this office and began to apply for other jobs. Rochdale Electricity department advertised for a clerk and with a hundred applicants he was invited to sit for a two-hour written examination. He and a local lad, Ronald Slater, were the only two candidates to have good marks and so were offered jobs which they took. But not long after this he was called up and joined the Royal Electrical and Mechanical Engineers where he was able to pursue his lifelong interest in electronics, working with radar for the duration of the war.

In September the two girls, Beryl and Sheila, started at one of the local schools. Beryl was at Rochdale High School. "It was a very unhappy time for me because I was so shy," she said later. "I found it hard to get used to the new life. The other girls laughed at the way I spoke and I got ragged a lot."

When they had left their home in Jersey the children had been told they could pack one toy. Beryl and Sheila both took their favourite dolls and they are still treasured today.

Beryl always remembered how much they longed to get back to Jersey throughout the war. "We talked about Jersey a great deal," she said. "This feeling of wanting to get back to Jersey lasted all my life but after the war I was carried along by events returned only for holidays." Her most memorable visit to Jersey occurred when her daughters arranged a surprise holiday and took her to stay at Eden Villa, Havre des Pas, the house where Beryl and her sister Sheila were born, which is still a guest house.

The only member of the family who returned to live in Jersey was Bryan who went back to work for the water company when his Army service ended.

Nine months after the family had moved into 17 St. Albans Street Mrs Cox, then aged 48, was taken ill and spent the next two and a half years in hospitals in Rochdale and Oswestry, Shropshire. Although absent from home, she remained the kingpin of the family, always encouraging, always optimistic. She died on 4 October, 1943. "It was a devastating blow," says Audrey. "A part of each one of us died with her." By this time Graeme and Ronald were in the Services. Beryl and Sheila were looked after by a family friend in Rochdale.

In addition to the 670 Channel Islanders who arrived in Rochdale on 22 June, a large number of Guernsey schoolchildren, accompanied only by their teachers, and other refugees, arrived in the town, as well as in the neighbouring towns of Bury, Burnley, Oldham and others. Some of their stories will be looked at in the next chapter.

After the war

17 St. Albans Street became the family home for the remainder of the war. By 1945 Beryl and Sheila were both working in Rochdale. Mr Cox remained in Rochdale until his death in June 1964.

After the war members of the family made enquiries about their furniture which they had left in the rented house in Jersey. They were told that in 1942 it had all been auctioned by the owner of the house and had realised £90. The owner had kept this money in lieu of the rent which it was considered should have been paid for the property from the time of their departure in June 1940.

Ronald and Bryan visited the house, 11 Duhamel Place, in 1947 to see if any of the family's possessions were still there but the house now had a new tenant and they was unable to recover anything except the rifle and the antique sword which Ronald had buried in the yard. The wooden butt had rotted away but the metal parts were still intact. A new butt was made for it and eventually it was given away in Jersey and is probably still in the island somewhere.

Chapter 5

Exodus of the Schools

The shock of having to leave home, family, friends and some cherished possessions all in the space of 24 hours had quickly to be replaced by action: a job to be done with no time to reflect. Yet, cycling down to school to take over my shift at the telephone, at 5.30 a.m. on that superb morning of June 20th I became suddenly, painfully, if only momentarily, aware of the loveliness of some beech trees. I was perhaps seeing them for the last time? It was a fleeting experience of being uprooted, and from deep down within my secret self there issued audible, involuntary groans! That memory remains vivid and sharp.

Miss Ella Mahy, one of the teachers at the Girls Intermediate
School, in a letter dated 11 September, 1990.

The Guernsey children who were separated from their parents and taken out of the island in 1940 might well wonder why other children in the Channel Islands were not treated in the same way. For many of the older children the evacuation with their school was a great adventure. Some had the time of their lives. Ten years later Michael Marshall even wrote a high-spirited novel about the adventures of himself and his school friends at Elizabeth College during their exile. (*The Small Army*) Another boy at the same college, Vernon G. Collenette, as an adult wrote a detailed historical account, *Elizabeth College in Exile, 1940-45*.

But for the youngest children, some no older than five, the evacuation and removal from their homes, was a deeply distressing and painful event. Margaret Brehaut, aged 5, was taken with the Amherst Infants' School (St Peter Port) to Glasgow. The one toy she was allowed to take was a favourite doll and she lost this on the long train journey. Today in her 60s, Mrs Brehaut says that the loss upset her greatly for a long time afterwards and she still feels bitter about it. Margaret Stedman (now Mrs Le Page), who was eight at the time, remembers the sense of confusion she had when, separated not only from her family but from an elder sister and a cousin, she was "crammed on a boat with lots of other children being sick." She too went to Glasgow where, although the local people were very kind, she felt abandoned. Today she speaks of the anguish she felt when an older girl at the school came up to a small group of little Guernsey children and said, "Now the Germans are in Guernsey and they've shot dead all your mummies and daddies."

Several weeks later an aunt collected her and took Margaret Stedman home to Southampton. She has memories only of frequent air raids, "little schooling and plenty nights in the shelter."

So why did the Guernsey authorities arrange the evacuation in this way?

The headlines in both the *Evening Press* and *The Star* emphasised in a dramatic way that all children were being hurriedly sent out of the island.

The events of that week remained vividly in the memories of many of these young evacuees. Some have as adults written movingly about their experiences.

Olive Quin was a young mother with a daughter of 18 months. In her book *The Long Goodbye*, she writes, 'We found scenes of panic in the schoolroom. Women and babies were crying, and many men were also in tears, as only women and children would be allowed to go on the boat.'

Yvonne Russell was a 15-year old schoolgirl, wrote 'The people who stayed called us cowards…It was all such a worry…We didn't really know if we were going to England or another country.' She had never been away from home and now her 'feelings were very mixed, excitement, fear of the unknown made me sick…'

The announcement in the *Evening Press* of 19 June was over the name of the Bailiff, Victor G. Carey. It gave the impression that the evacuation of children was compulsory. A headline PARENTS MUST REPORT THIS EVENING was followed by the opening sentences 'Arrangements are being made for the evacuation of (1) children of school age and (2) children under school age to reception areas in the United Kingdom under Government arrangement. The evacuation is expected to take place tomorrow, the 20th June 1940.'

Only in a later sentence was there a hint that the evacuation was not compulsory. 'Parents of schoolchildren are to attend at the school attended by their children at 7 p.m. today to notify their willingness or otherwise for the evacuation of their children.'

Writing shortly after the war, Mrs Cortvriend probably expressed what most parents felt at the time. 'Our decision that our children must go was made irrevocably from the first moment we had heard that the opportunity was available.'

Exact figures are not available but it was estimated at the time that of 6500 children on the registers of Guernsey schools, 4,700 travelled from Guernsey in school parties with 500 teachers and voluntary helpers on 20-21 June. This left 1,800 children remaining in Guernsey, but of these about 800 evacuated with their parents. In a census of Guernsey on 27 July 1940 the school population (ages from 6-13) was recorded as 1,011 (460 males and 551 females) This was slightly less than a figure for school registrations of 1,051 published in Guernsey's *Evening Press* of 8 July 1940.

These figures contrast with Jersey, where, if children evacuated, they went with members of their family, not as a school party, and the school population during the Occupation was estimated to have been about 4,500.

The notices which appeared in Guernsey newspapers on 20 June listed in detail the clothing which children should take with them.

Articles to take

Children should take with them on evacuation the following articles:
Gas masks, Two ration books (current and new one).
Besides the clothes which the child will be wearing, which should include an overcoat or mackintosh, a complete change of clothing should be carried. The following is suggested:
Girls: One vest or combination, one pair of knickers, one bodice, one petticoat, two pairs of stocking, Handkerchiefs, Slip and blouse, Cardigan.
Boys: One vest, one shirt with collar, one pair of pants, one pullover or jersey, one pair of knickers, handkerchiefs, two pairs of socks or stockings.
Additional for all: Night attire, comb, towel, soap, face-cloth, tooth-brush, and, if possible, boots and shoes and plimsolls. Blankets must not be taken.
The Rations: Rations for the journey: Sandwiches (egg or cheese); Packets of nuts and seedless raisins; Dry biscuits (with little packets of cheese); Barley sugar (rather than chocolate); Apple; Orange.   *Official instructions published in Guernsey's newspapers; 19 June 1940*

In the case of Elizabeth College the boys were given a hurriedly prepared typewritten list to take home. This included 'a satchel of books,...mug, plate, knife fork and spoon,' but omitted to mention a towel. The only luggage that could be taken had to be carried by the boys themselves so the college was unable to take any equipment. The omission of the towel was to cost the school a financial penalty. From the small amount of money the head had available when they arrived in England, they bought 300 new towels.

It was decided that the first to embark on 20 June should be the younger children at schools in St Peter Port because the town was thought more likely to be attacked and it would be better if the younger ones were on the ships which travelled by day. A message had been received from England that three ships with a capacity of 2,000 children would arrive at 2 a.m. on the morning of 20 June. By 4 a.m. 1,900 children from most of the town schools with their teachers were assembling on the quay, having walked in long lines through the town in the darkness. However the first of the ships, the *Antwerp*, did not arrive until about 9 a.m. so the children had to wait for several hours. The first children to embark were from Amherst School, St Sampson's and St Joseph's Boys. The *Antwerp* sailed at about 10 a.m. with 1,154 passengers, children, teachers and helpers. Fortunately most of the children were too young to realise the seriousness of what was happening and most seemed to be looking forward to the journey with eagerness. The weather, calm and warm, was especially favourable.

The next ship to arrive that morning was the *Felixstowe* and this sailed with 434 passengers, mainly children from Vauvert Boys' and Girls' Schools. Next was the *Carina*, a collier in such a dirty condition that the Secretary of the Education Council, Mr A. Winterflood, who was in charge of these embarkations, decided not to use her. British troops were embarking at the same time and there was some anxiety that German aircraft might appear and attack the harbour so Winterflood persuaded the Sea Transport Officer to commandeer the *Haslemere* which had just arrived. This was done and the remaining 300 children embarked at 11 a.m. but she could not get up steam again until 2.00 p.m. and then sailed for Weymouth.

Meanwhile Elizabeth College had assembled as usual and the boys were then sent home to collect their luggage and to say fare-well to their parents. Unfortunately there was no firm news about the times of the arrival of the evacuation ships. They could arrive at any time so the school had to wait, ready to move off at short notice. Because of the fine weather they were able to sit on their suitcases in the grounds of the College. They waited all day . News was received by the Education Council that a ship was expected at 9 p.m. and the College was told in the evening that they could embark at 10 p.m.

At 9.30 they began to march to the harbour. Some of their luggage was loaded on to two or three vans whose drivers had volunteered to help but many had to carry their suitcases. Vernon Collenette, one of the 150 boys on the march, wrote later that 'it must have seemed a pathetic procession that made its way slowly down St Julian's Avenue, halting occasionally to rest in obedience to blasts from a whistle carried by the Principal.'

The *Batavier IV* arrived at 10 p.m. She was a Dutch cargo vessel of 1,570 tons, built in 1902, which had been on the London-Rotterdam line and had very little accommodation for passengers but it was decided that she could take 800. Officials began to count the children as they were on a gangway but after a time it was realised that some were going aboard on a second gangway and were not being counted so the attempt to control the number was abandoned. Finally, when it was estimated that there were about 800 aboard, including teachers and helpers, she sailed at midnight.

The other schools on the *Batavier* included the Ladies College (about 100 girls) and pupils of the two States Intermediate schools. It was an uncomfortable journey. Many of the boys were crowded into the holds, some of which were still littered with straw from a cargo of cattle.

By dawn land could be seen on the horizon but the ship's progress seemed very slow. It dropped anchor in the roads outside Weymouth and it was not until the early afternoon that the children had disembarked and were standing on the Weymouth quay.

The next ship to leave Guernsey was the *Sheringham* (900 tons). She had been to Alderney on the 19 June where she had picked up 76 children, almost all the pupils from the two schools on the island, the Convent School and St Anne's. It was decided that the *Sheringham* could take 750 children and would sail early on the morning of 21 June so the children of Vale and Torteval schools were asked to assemble at 3 a.m. However when Mr Winterflood arrived at the quay at 3.30 a.m. to supervise the loading he found that because the tide was low the gangway was inclined too steeply for young children, all of whom were under 12 and some as young as five years. Later he wrote, 'However the ship's officers and crew were very helpful and managed to get the gangway down on to a lower landing.'

The children arrived in semi-darkness and had to descend wet and slippery steps. Mr Winterflood reported later 'more than 600 juniors and infants embarked without a mishap of any kind.'

At 4.30 a.m. another steamer, the 2,000 ton *Viking*, arrived. She was biggest ship (over 2,000 tons) so far used and her master said he could take several thousand children. 1,880 embarked on this vessel soon after 5 a.m. She sailed at 9 a.m. and would have sailed earlier but for the fact that by this time many parents were having second thoughts about letting their children go and there were a number of arguments because of this. 'Were there enough lifeboats on the ship?' 'Would the ship be convoyed?' 'Where would the children be living?' These and many other questions either had negative replies, or could not be answered.

The *Duke of York* also arrived in Guernsey early in the morning of 21 June but the last batches of schoolchildren had been able to get on the *Viking* so the *Duke of York* was used to evacuate children under school age accompanied by their mothers. Later that day she sailed with about 2,000 mothers and young children on board, including about 700 babies.

Mrs Cortvriend, who remained in the island and did not hear from her 14-year old daughter until there was a Red Cross message in the following year, wrote that some parents,

> ...driven to desperation by the suspense, took their children home
> again; others, torn by indecision, changed their minds three or four
> times over, taking their children home, and bringing them back
> again...the organisers were greatly handicapped by the constantly
> changing numbers to be arranged for and escorted.. Many of the
> parents were influenced by neighbours and friends, and often the
> withdrawal of a child in one locality would be followed by a whole
> group from the same neighbourhood.

Children on the *Viking* came from the following schools: Hautes Capelles, Castel, St Martin's, St Peter's, Les Eturs, Kingsley House, Morely, St Saviour's, Sarel, Seward, Forest, Delancey R.C., St Joseph's Girls and Infants, Blanchelande, La Chaumiere, The Convent, Cordier Hill, Les Cotils, Froebel, L'Islet, and Les Vauxbelets.

Considering that such a large number of children were involved with this sudden evacuation it is noteworthy that very little official information on the subject was published either during or after the war. The Secretary of the States Education Council, A. Winterflood, wrote a report during the following week (28 June 1940) but this was not released to the public until 1988, and even then it is believed that the name of a teacher who deserted was deleted. This lapse of duty may have arisen for an unavoidable reason such as illness but the fact that names of teacher and school have been deleted from an old document has given rise to suspicion and rumour. Most of the records of the Education Council were not preserved after the war and the main sources of information available today are the personal reminiscences of those involved.

The plans for the reception of refugees at Weymouth and in the northern towns did not provide for large numbers of unaccompanied children. The quays and the railway station were overcrowded with refugees from Jersey too, but most of these were families with adults.

Eventually a train was allocated to the Guernsey children. It left Weymouth at 5 p.m. One of the boys on this train kept a note of the stations and the times the train passed them: 5.20 Dorchester, 6.05 Yeovil, 6.50 Westbury South, 6.55 Trowbridge, 7.02 Bradford on Avon, 7.13 Bath, 7.28 Bristol (where they were given bottles of water, milk and lemonade)7.58 entered Severn tunnel, 8.18 Newport, train stopped to take in water at Hereford and many boys got out and filled bottles with water. After this he dozed off but later noted that the train passed through Crewe, Chester and Manchester, then up to Rochdale before coming south to Oldham, where they arrived at 3.50 am on Sat 22 June. The rail journey had taken 10 3⁄4 hours and the total journey was 21 1⁄4 hours.

The northern reception

Oldham council officials had been warned that refugees were on their way. Trams and buses were waiting at the station. The girls of the Ladies College were taken to the Baptist Sunday School in King Street where the ladies of the WVS had refreshments waiting. In a large hall upstairs the WVS had covered the floor with palliasses and after the tiring journey most of the girls slept until the following morning. Meanwhile the boys of Elizabeth College and the Intermediate were taken in buses to the hall of the Oldham Industrial Co-operative Society where the WVS also had refreshments and temporary beds waiting. The girls of the Intermediate School were taken to Rochdale.

In the days which followed some of the children were fetched by parents who had managed to leave Guernsey and by relatives but a large majority remained in the care of their teachers. Michael Marshall who was 14 at the time, wrote later that 'Free trips to the boating lake, swimming baths and cinemas helped to take their minds off more unpleasant things – the separation from their families and news of the ruthless bombing of their island home. Not knowing whether his parents were alive or dead, Marsh was desperately unhappy. He sobbed quietly in the refuge of the lavatory and mopped his eyes with toilet paper because he had not brought a handkerchief in the confusion of the flight.'

Refugee children, still with their labels, being taken to their billets in Eccles, Manchester

The Principal of Elizabeth College, the Rev. William Henry Goodenough Milnes, made strenuous efforts by contacting the local education authority and visiting Government departments in London to obtain premises which the school could occupy as a unit. But the official policy was that refugee children must be billeted in private homes and absorbed by local schools.

It was fortunate that one of the members of Elizabeth College staff happened to know that the Unitarian Church maintained some holiday homes at Great Hucklow, a village in Derbyshire, about 12 miles west of Sheffield. Within a week, and partly because of the good will that existed on all sides, arrangements were made for Elizabeth College and the Ladies College to move to Great Hucklow. The Ladies College remained here throughout the summer of 1940 but the premises were cramped and had no suitable classroom accommodation.

In August the Board of Education reported that classrooms were available for the girls at Howell's School, Denbigh, a well known public school in north Wales. The girls would have to be billeted in the town but this was considered preferable to remaining at Great Hucklow. In September 63 girls, all that remained with the teachers of the 100 who had left Guernsey, moved to Denbigh. They were delighted with the fine buildings and large playing-field of their new school. The girls fitted in well with the educational facilities of Howell's School and the

65

Ladies College remained there until July 1945. The billeting arrangements did not always work smoothly and this gave the staff problems. In addition they had the major problem of clothing for the girls. Some girls were helped by relatives but the majority relied on the College to help them. As with many other CI evacuees they received much help from the clothing depots set up by the Channel Islands Refugees Committee, described in another chapter.

In Great Hucklow the boys of Elizabeth College Junior Department were housed in several corrugated iron huts on a slope overlooking the village. These had been used in peacetime for weekend camps for boys from big northern cities. The senior boys were housed in the premises of the Lancashire and Derbyshire Gliding Club which were about half a mile from the village on top of a plateau which was partly a flying field. The accommodation was fairly primitive. An outhouse which was called a 'bathroom' contained only a tin bath, a copper for heating water and a few wash-basins. When bathing was in progress the hot water was poured into the bath and the boys were not allowed more than three minutes in the water before they were rinsed with cold water thrown over them by the next in the queue.

Most of the staff at this time were housed in the village or at Tideswell, a small town about two miles away. The Rev. and Mrs Milnes occupied a caravan.

An unusual asset in the village of Great Hucklow was a barn which had been converted into a theatre known as The Playhouse. One of the problems for the staff of both Elizabeth College and the Ladies College was to keep their charges occupied during the summer holidays of 1940. Some of the pupils had been able to live with relatives elsewhere in the country but a substantial number remained at Great Hucklow. Although the hardships of the time are not forgotten in the reminiscences of boys and staff it is clear that many had a companionable and happy time engaged in a production of Twelfth Night at this theatre. It was the first time that girls of the Ladies College had co-operated with Elizabeth College in a theatrical production and five girls took the women's parts. Not only were the actors in the play kept busy in the preparations but there were opportunities for the boys to be stage-hands, to paint scenery, to work as electricians, and in advertising and selling tickets. The first rehearsal was on 19 July and the first public performance on 15 August. Performances were given throughout that week to large and appreciative audiences from the surrounding countryside and then at the end of August the company gave four performances at the Buxton Playhouse, about nine miles away. The proceeds from all this amounted to about £140, a substantial sum which helped the two schools greatly.

The boys were fascinated by the nearby moors. The wide and hilly countryside around Great Hucklow, so different from that of their island home, was a stimulating new experience for most of them They were able to take up many new outdoor activities. During that summer they took long walks, exploring the Kinderscout area and visiting the Peak Cavern, Peveril Castle and the Blue John mine at Castleton.

Some boys remember that they always believed that the war would end soon

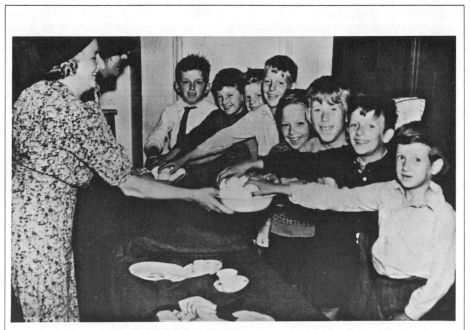

Above: Pictures of 'happy Channel Island refugee children' were often posed. This one was in the Daily Sketch.
Below: Another posed picture of CI children in June 1940 with the toys given them on arrival (Daily Sketch).

and they would not be there for very long. Michael Marshall tells in *The Small Army* that some boys were always thinking of ways that they might get to Guernsey. One idea was to get hold of a barrage balloon and use it to carry a canoe across the Channel so that they could lower themselves into the sea and paddle ashore in Guernsey.

Not having any equipment for cricket, or a suitable ground, they began to play baseball on the flying field, although this was brought to an end on 25th August when a German aircraft dropped bombs nearby. There was no casualty but it was thought the Germans might be targeting the flying field and the Principal decided it would be unwise to use it again for baseball.

Although it was a relatively carefree summer for the boys the Rev Milnes and his senior staff were much preoccupied with their search for more permanent school premises. The buildings they occupied at Great Hucklow were not heated and unsuitable for winter use. Should they go back to Oldham or a similar urban area where the boys could be billeted and attend local schools? Or should they try to find suitable premises at which the College could maintain its own identity?

Rev Milnes very much wanted to maintain the College as an independent unit and it was clearly because of his energy in this direction that after finding a large and suitable vacant house called Whitehall, problems of finance and a certain amount of official opposition were overcome. Whitehall was in a rural setting about three miles from Buxton. By 30 September 1940 the senior forms had settled in to what was to be their home until they returned to Guernsey in 1945. Whitehall was leased with 37 acres of pasture and woodland. The junior forms remained in the satisfactory permanent buildings of a hostel in Great Hucklow belonging to the Rev C. Peach.

To finance the move the College had received a number of donations from Old Elizabethans and friends in the UK. A committee consisting of Messrs. W.H.G. Milnes (the Principal) R.T. Ozanne, L.R. Cohen, E.G. Fleming, V.A. Grantham and Dr. F. Hardy was formed to guarantee the cost of the Whitehall Estate.

Whitehall was in some ways an ideal place for a school but there was not enough space. The class-rooms were used as dining-rooms. Books were removed at mealtimes so that cauldrons of stew and large bowls of rice-pudding could be brought in.

Some teachers were unhappy because their salaries had been reduced. In October 1941 two wrote to the Channel Islands Refugees Committee in London to appeal for help. They complained that they had been unjustly treated 'when salaries were readjusted in England.' They said that the terms of their contract with the College were not being carried out and they were worried that their pensions would be prejudiced. The CIRC passed the complaint to the Ministry of Education.

Meanwhile the girls of the States Intermediate School who had gone to Rochdale were given temporary accommodation in Roylelands, one of several houses taken over for refugees by Rochdale council. In the next chapter the diary of one of these girls, Diana Falla, describes the daily life at Roylelands. Kathleen Cowling, who was 12 at the time, wrote as an adult,

> Living at Roylelands was difficult for everyone. We each had a camp-bed, blankets, a sleeping bag, and, if we were lucky, a pillow. We all took turns with the housework, and, as we were considered the senior section of the school, one day a week was spent at Horse Carrs, a house where the junior girls lived, to assist with their laundry. Rooms had to be cleaned of course but there were no vacuum cleaners. Instead we used dustpans and brushes with damp tea-leaves to lay the dust.
>
> Our main cooked meal of the day was brought in containers by 'dinner ladies.' We were fortunate in having teachers who stayed with us throughout the war and provided some continuity in our lives.

Eventually most of the girls were billeted in private homes but they did not have to go through the notorious selection procedure of lining up and being chosen by householders.

The senior girls of the Intermediate attended Castleton Senior School in Rochdale, where they had separate classrooms. Juniors had their own classrooms at Greenbank Junior School.

Local newspapers often reported items with a Channel Island interest. An outsider might have had the impression that the Channel Island people had introduced some new culture to Rochdale. By early 1941 the girls of the Intermediate School were reported to be giving musical concerts with 'numbers in English, French and Guernsey patois.' On one occasion, 'Miss Winifred Roughton, the singing mistress, charmed the large audience with her pianoforte solos and her sister Miss N. H. Roughton, headmistress, with her solos, proved herself a violinist of much ability.'

Miss Roughton personally knew Uncle Mac, the famous BBC broadcaster, and through him a programme of singing and music by the girls of the Intermediate school was broadcast in Children's Hour on 27 May 1941.

The winter of 1940-41 was a particularly cold one and many of the Guernsey children experienced snow for the first time. Kathleen Cowling remembers,

> The first snow of that winter was very exciting and I was still young enough to enjoy it. Deep drifts of snow and snowball fights were great fun. We used to walk home from school the long way so that we could follow the course of the frozen brook.

The boys of the Intermediate School remained in Oldham where they merged with Hulme Grammar School on 28 October 1940. It seems to have been a happy and productive time for many of them. Some won scholarships to Elizabeth

College. Many had excellent relationships with foster parents. After the war one boy wrote that he '...finally went to stay with the very nice couple who looked after me until the end of the war.' In 1942 he was introduced to Bourne Street Methodist Church where he made lots of friends and enjoyed joining in the social activities. He remembered the Sunday walks around Daisy Nook and the outings they had on the moors. They often travelled by tram from Hollinwood to Manchester to hear classical concerts, and had one memorable visit to Belle Vue Circus.

He left school in July 1943 and started work at Ferranti's general office in Hollinwood, on 27 Sept. In April 1945 he was called up and started training as a Bevin Boy. After a month's training in Manchester he was sent to Chamber Colliery, Hollinwood on 24th May. In July he applied to go back to Guernsey and to his surprise he was given permission within two weeks and he returned to Guernsey on 18 August, considering himself lucky to be included in the Intermediate school party which travelled on that day.

Pupils of Castel School (Guernsey) at Warburton, Cheshire, in 1942.

SCHOLARSHIP EXAMINATION, 1943.

For children evacuated from Guernsey, Alderney and Sark.

JUNE 22nd, 1943.

ARITHMETIC

10-5—11-15 a.m.

1. Add 98 ; 102 ; 73 ; 127 ; 51 ; 49.

2. Divide each of these three numbers by 25.
   400 ; 3200 ; 750.

3. Add 49 times 16 to 51 times 16.

4. Divide 12,987 by 13.

5. Multiply 888 by 1,001.

6.   (*a*) $1\frac{1}{2} + \frac{4}{5} + 1\frac{1}{4}$.
     (*b*) $6\frac{1}{4} - 1\frac{5}{8}$.

7. A merchant buys 20 hams for 14s. each, and sells them at 17s. each. How much does he gain?

8. My billet is 5 furlongs 11 yards from school. Tell me in yards how far this distance is short of one mile.

9. If 9 cricket bats cost £6 15s. 0d., what would 20 cost?

10. The area of a tennis court is 312 sq. yds. ; it is 12 yds. wide. Find its length, and its perimeter (distance round).

11. At a sale a lady bought 5 yards of cloth for 12s. 6d. The cloth had been reduced 6d. a yard. How much a yard was it before the sale?

12. A Guernsey farmer had 4 cows. One gave 3 qts. 1 pt. of milk, another 1 gall. 2 qts., and the other two 1 gallon each. How much did the four cows give altogether?

13. The Guernsey Mailboat sailing to Southampton carried the following :—
    39 ship's crew, 304 men, 358 women, and 299 children.
        Find (*a*) How many on board altogether?
              (*b*) How many grown up passengers?
              (*c*) How many more grown up passengers than children?

14. I left my house in St. Peter Port one morning at 9 o'clock, and walked to Vazon in 1 hour 15 mins. Then I bathed and played on the sands for one hour and a half. I rode home on the La Rapide Bus, which passes my door, and arrived back at noon. How long did I spend riding on the bus?

Victoria College, Jersey

As has been mentioned in an earlier chapter the Jersey authorities did not favour the evacuation of schools *en bloc*. However a number of children left the island with their parents and 14 boys of Victoria College who were about to sit examinations also left the island with four members of the staff, including the headmaster, J.H. Grummitt. The examination candidates spent five weeks at Shrewsbury School. During the summer the Board of Education suggested they should join Elizabeth College, but this was rejected and eventually about 40 boys joined Bedford School. By 1941 they were well established as a school within a school and were known as 'Victoria College at Bedford.' In that year seven boys were boarders at the school, 22 were billeted in Bedford, and eight lived with their parents in Bedford. The Channel Islands Refugees Committee gave financial support and the College also benefited from private donations. A well-produced newsletter was published regularly and circulated widely among Old Victorians in the services and elsewhere.

Other schools

There is not the space here to describe in detail what happened to each school which was evacuated. Some children were collected soon after arrival in England by their parents or other relatives. Others were found family homes and then joined a local school.

Guernsey teachers remained with their pupils but at a meeting on 28 July 1940 between CI representatives and the Ministry of Health in London to discuss the problems the two Guernsey Colleges were having in finding accommodation it the Ministry decided there were too many Channel Island teachers for the number of CI children and some teachers would have to be made redundant and placed on the national register of unemployed teachers. Financial help was offered by the National Union of Teachers but it did not compensate for the separation and dislocation they must have felt.

Although considered a "safe" area the north of England suffered numerous air-raids and some Channel Islanders lost their lives or were injured. In one case a Guernsey boy of 11, John Lainé, billeted in Oldham, was in bed at midnight on 12 October 1941 when the house was hit by a bomb and he was buried under the debris. He was rescued after several hours but the local boy of the same age who shared the bedroom was killed.

And apart from the frequent air-raids the dark cloud which hung over nearly all these schoolchildren was the lack of information about parents and other relatives who had remained in Guernsey. Richard Walker who was at the Intermediate School in Oldham remembers the rumours which spread rapidly on 29 June about the air-raids in Guernsey. And then he was called aside by the headmaster to be told that a Home Office telegram had been received saying that

You are invited to the Civic Reception and the opening of 'We'll meet again', an exhibition to commemorate the evacuation of the 'Guernsey boys' to Oldham on 22nd June 1940.

22nd JUNE 1990 at 7.30 p.m.

To be opened by the Worshipful the Mayor Cllr. Sid Jacobs J.P. supported by Mr. Rex Carrè, former Guernsey boy and Headmaster of the Bluecoat School.

To be held in Oldham Art Gallery, Union Street, Oldham. Exhibition organised by the Local Interest Museum.

Oldham Leisure Services

The boys of the Intermediate School made a long-lasting impression on Oldham. In June, 1990, fifty years after their arrival, an exhibition to commemorate the event was mounted at the Oldham Museum. The organiser, Mrs Freda Millett, went to considerable trouble to locate surviving "boys" as well as their local foster parents. On 22 June, 1990 a reception was held in the Oldham Art Gallery in the presence of the Mayor, Councillor Sid Jacobs, JP, and Mr Rex Carré, a former Guernsey boy who has recently retired as headmaster of the Bluecoat School, Oldham.

Over 100 people were present. Mrs Millett says, "It was quite moving to see people recognise each other once again and to witness the obvious joy they experienced when seeing the exhibition. Bonds were formed again and friendships renewed."

The boys pictured in the invitation (illustrated) are the Guernsey twins, David and John Davison. They were billeted during the war with Dr. Walker and his wife, who was the children's officer for Oldham. Both boys went back to Guernsey after the Liberation and then returned to England to go to University. John qualified in medicine and joined the practice of his foster parent, Dr Walker. David qualified as a dentist and still lives in the north of England.

his father had been killed in the harbour raid. By this time all lines to the island had been cut so he was not even able to communicate with his mother.

Despite these and many other hardships the letters, articles and reminiscences which have been written by the evacuees, and particularly those who were brought to England in school parties, offer deeply felt thanks to the towns which received them. The voluntary helpers of the WVS come in for particular praise. They were not only waiting to give sustenance and help to the arrivals at Weymouth and in the northern towns but gave constant daily help in all kinds of ways in the years that followed.

By the end of 1940 the Boys' Intermediate School, now attached to the Hulme Grammar School in Oldham, was already publishing its school magazine and the words of the headmaster in the December issue make a fitting end to this chapter:

> It was no fun to be turned out of our homes and our homeland at such short notice, to leave our parents behind, to cross a perilous sea, to face the great unknown, and literally to be sent into exile, leaving an island where we were serenely happy and very content, an Island renowned for its sunlit seas and glorious scenery, its warmth and beauty, its ease and serenity, its calm and peacefulness, but our sadness has been brightened, our burden lightened; our parting eased, our stress appeased; our exile sweetened, our gratitude deepened; by your warm reception and generous hospitality.

Above: Guernsey girls at Marple, Cheshire, receiving clothing supplied by American sympathisers.

Guernsey has no reason to be ashamed of its system of elementary education. Arising from the evacuation of the elementary schools three points have given much satisfaction. First, the standard of attainment of these children is at least equal to that of the children in the United Kingdom. Secondly, its elementary school buildings compare favourable with those to be found in corresponding districts in Britain. And thirdly, Guernsey schools are provided with far more school equipment than schools in similar localities in the United Kingdom.

from *Nos Iles* (London, 1944)

Why I want to go home

I am 13 years of age, and I came over to England, with my mother and younger brother, during the evacuation in 1940. The reason why I want to return to Guernsey is because my father and grandfather are there, and I still look upon it as my home and everything that word means. Many of my friends are still there, whom I would very much like to see again, also the greenhouses and the narrow country lanes for which this island is noted.

Another reason why I wish to return is because I miss the rich Guernsey milk and butter which is supposed to be the richest obtainable. Guernsey cattle are noted all over the world, and a few years ago Americans were buying all the cattle they could in Guernsey.

The climate of this island is much milder than here. I also miss the blue sea of Guernsey very much, which I was able to see every day, and enjoy bathing facilities. I have seen many beautiful places in England and Wales, and I have enjoyed myself very much like the man, Sir Walter Scott, who wrote the poem, from which the following are the first few lines: "Breathes there the man with soul so dead who never to himself has said, This is my own, my native land."

Within a couple of years I will be seeking employment, and I should very much like to do something in Guernsey to obliterate the ugliness which has been caused by military fortifications and to restore the island to its former beauty of a gem set in a silver sea. These are my reasons for wanting to return, and I have every reason to believe I shall be able to return in the very near future.

(This essay by Herbert White of Cardiff won first prize in a competition organised in 1944 by the Bristol Channel Islands Association.)

SARK

Sometimes when I'm in London in my thoughts I'm far away,
Strolling down the little lane that leads to Dixcart Bay;
I travel there on wishes, across the watery miles
That lie between Southampton and the lovely Channel Isles.
The noises of the city beat harshly on the ear;
I'd rather hear the breaking of the waters green and clear,
The waves that fling their silver spray 'gainst rocks so grim and stark,
the surging of the restless sea around the Isle of Sark.
Someday I'll be returning to that beloved shore,
And from the little harbour I shall climb the hill once more,
And see the fishing nets spread out to dry upon the grass,
And smell the honeysuckle in the hedges as I pass.

Robert Dawson-Freer, November 1942

THE ALDERNEY FARMER

(The following is part of a verse that began on 23 June 1940. It was
completed in January, 1945 and sold at 3d per copy on behalf of the
Alderney Relief Committee.)

For him the happy life he loved so well
Was ended, when he left his home that June;
His agony of mind he did not tell
To any, save himself in silent gloom
At dawn that day he felt himself secure,
By noon he knew he was a ruined man;
His all was gone, and now he was obscure,
A homeless refugee without a plan.
His farm was rough outside but neat within,
And full of comfort 'gainst the winter's blast;
Enough and more for all his Kith & Kin,
To see them through life's journey to the last
The last lines:
"Five years have passed, Ah me!" I hear him sigh;
But 'twas only Au Revoir you said that June,
'twas not Good-Bye!

by E. Parry

Chapter 6

Diana's Diary

Roylelands is a large house standing back from the Manchester Road. The rooms are large and airy. The late owner was Mr K. Menzies. The staff have two bathrooms so we have to queue for washing. The rooms took a lot of keeping clean. The rose garden was on the verge of collapse and the vegetable garden is a mass of weeds. The lawn is quite nice.

Undated entry in diary

Diana June Falla was only 12 when she left Guernsey with the States Intermediate School. When she arrived in Rochdale she began to keep a daily journal. For such a young child the diary is remarkably down-to-earth and objective. She continued to keep a diary until October, 1943.

Her parents were still in Guernsey but they are hardly mentioned in the diary. It is the small domestic details, particularly the meals, which she records. As the diary progresses it seems likely that because she could not communicate with her parents the daily notes she made were a substitute for the letters she would have sent to them. They were clearly and neatly written in ink in a new notebook (175 x 225 mm). In adult life Diana became a sculptress and the diary contains evidence of a talent for drawing and painting. On 9 July she was unwell and had to remain in bed but she filled her time by sketching the view from the bedroom window. Two coloured sketches on cartridge paper are with the diary. In one can be seen the back of Rochdale's imposing Town Hall, with other buildings clearly recognisable. The other is a coloured sketch of the front of Roylelands. This can now be compared with a photograph from a similar viewpoint and is clearly an accurate representation. When a lady doctor attended her in Rochdale, Diana was amused by the doctor's showy hats so she sketched them in the diary.

The first entry is headed 20 June 1940 but it is unlikely that Diana wrote it on that day. She probably began it on Sunday, 23 June, her second day in Rochdale. After that there were daily entries until she left Rochdale on 23 July 1940.

In the following transcript her spelling has been corrected but otherwise it remains as she wrote it. In a few places I have added words in square brackets to clarify her meaning.

20 June 1940: We set off from the school at 9 p.m. and after a lot of fuss got on the boat at midnight. [The boat] set off at about 12.25. We had to go down in the hold with the Girls College. It was dreadfully hot and stuffy. We had to sleep in our lifebelts. It was very uncomfortable. We sailed on a Dutch tramp Batavier IV. The crew was composed of French, English and Dutch sailors. The boys (Intermediate and College) went to the forepart of the ship, and we went down into the afterhold.

We had to sleep on the floor which was extremely uncomfortable. Although relatives promised a nice crossing, it was very rough. I only dozed all night. We could have gone up on deck at any time. Some of the girls went up and the crew gave them coffee. They were very sick. Lots of people were ill but luckily I kept all right. At about 7.30 a.m. the sea calmed down for we were nearing Portland Bill. Not very far from land we sighted the stern of a Norwegian wood ship protruding from the water. It had evidently been sunk. We saw about 50 destroyers, cruisers, submarines, etc. We were going very slowly but soon we saw some merchant ships. We counted 22 ships waiting to be convoyed. One ship was Dutch from Rotterdam called Sytad Mehrmitch. Most of the ships were English or French. We eventually got alongside but we were not allowed to land so we sat down and ate our dinner. After about an hour we were allowed to land (this was at 12.45 p.m...) We had to walk a good way up the pier. Then we had to wait for a long time outside the theatre on the pier. We were medically examined. As I was all right I was ticketed. Then we walked into the town into a large hall surrounded by gardens. There we were given biscuits, sandwiches and tea by the Women's Voluntary Service and the Sea Scouts. By this time we were very tired. Some buses came and took us to the station at 5 p.m. It was boiling hot. After 30 minutes we got on the train and we left at about 6 o'clock. We were 8 in a compartment. Miss Brittain was with us and she was a sport. We all tried to sleep but gave it up. The country we passed through was lovely. Although the train was a special we made two or three stops. We had quite a good tea when the train stopped at Bristol. We tried to go to sleep four on the floor and four on the seats. Unfortunately I was on the floor. In the middle of the night Diana Wallis began sleep-walking but after nearly knocking herself out she calmed down. After a long uncomfortable night we arrived at Rochdale at 6 a.m. On the way we saw five barrage balloons. One looked as though it had been pricked. We saw three coming down They looked very silvery. In the train I wrote to Miss Wilson.

22 June: At Rochdale we had to wait on the station for about fifteen minutes. Then we went in buses to Roylelands. It was pouring with rain. We thought it awful but afterwards learnt that [rain] was a very common occurrence. After a short bus ride we arrived at a big brick house with a long drive. We were all given soup and sandwiches and then put to bed for three hours. For dinner we had lamb and beans and then some awful custard. We chatted, etc. all the afternoon. At 6 p.m. we had a tea of bread and jam., then some lovely strawberries. They were a present from a nursery. After that we went to bed. I went to sleep first and had a very comfortable night. Our beds were borrowed from the A.R.P. We later learnt that all the food was given from the town's stores by the Mayor. It came ready cooked in a van from a communal kitchen. The town gave us the food for a month without ration cards.

23 June: Today we had bananas for breakfast. We then went for a walk through narrow dirty streets past a very old church, through a black farm past a large pond through a deserted factory and on to the downs where we had a rest. For dinner we had pie and sago pudding. No sugar! After dinner we read, wrote, or played games.[At 3 p.m. we went] to St Aidan's parish Church. It was quite a nice service. It looked very like St Andrews. It was very plain inside. The vicar had a very queer voice. In the early evening Miss Clayton took our money into the 'bank.' For tea we had a lovely fruit salad. We danced until lights out.

24 June: It was lovely weather (for a change) and after bread and butter breakfast Miss Brittain took us across some wasteland to a park with a lake in the middle. We had great fun going down slides, on swings, etc. (including Miss Brittain). We went back to a dinner of sausages and mash and then for dessert ginger pudding and nice custard. Having had dinner we read or played games in the garden until the M.O.H.[doctor] arrived. She was awfully nice. I was all right, thank goodness. After this the W.V.S. registered us. For tea we had lettuce and tomatoes and after playing in the garden we went to bed and read, talked or sang until the whistle (lights out) and then sleep if you were lucky.

25 June: At 1.20 a.m. we were awakened by the air raid siren. I was rather dazed at first but I soon grabbed shoes, gas mask and coat and followed the crowd down to the empty wine cellar.

Everyone chatted although we could hear the guns. As far as we knew Jerry did not drop any [bombs]. After 50 minutes we went back to bed. We wakened later than usual in the morning and we had bread and margarine for breakfast. After breakfast we went into a field by the Dunlop factory to play rounders with Miss Sayer. Then we went back and I wrote my diary. For dinner we had shepherd's pie and haricot beans, then prunes and custard (very good). For tea we had lettuce and tomatoes. The lettuces were brought to us by some boys from the plots at the back of the house. These plots are run by the Dunlop people. After tea we mucked around again till a lovely sandwich and milk supper. By the way the weather hasn't been at all bad and in some cases lovely.

26 June: After washing and eating a bread and jam breakfast I joyfully found I had two letters, one from Miss Wilson and one from mummy and daddy. The seniors are moving to Boothroyd across the road. Went straight to Horse Carrs (the other side of the town). We have to do some housework to help everyone. We had no work in the morning but I swept in the afternoon. Some others went to the [public] baths. For tea we had cherries and strawberries and I had seven letters, birthday cards mostly and two postal orders for 5/- each. Miss Mahy wished me many happy returns of tomorrow. Some kind person bought us dozens of books and games and some scouts bought us some tennis rackets and cricket bats. At the moment I am sitting on my bed writing this (I am very happy). We went to bed and except for suffering from cold feet...

27 June: [Diana's 13th birthday] I awoke to a lovely morning at 5 a.m. and read until breakfast. Nearly everyone wished me 'many happy returns of the day.' At breakfast I had a letter from Auntie Marie and Marion including a postal order for 2/6d. Miss Sayer changed all my postal orders and I gave them into the bank [run by Miss Clayton]. I worked in the morning [housework?]. We had pie for dinner and then bananas cooked in custard. After dinner some people went to the [public] baths but we went to the park and had a fine time going down the slides and swinging. It is a very nice park with a lake with an island in the middle. It is about half a mile from Roylelands. We had bananas for tea and I had three telegrams. It was a lovely surprise. Here is a list of my presents and telegrams:

Presents at home [Guernsey]

Mummy & Daddy	5/-	pyjama set; 2 omnibus books
Marjorie & Jack	5/-	pyjama set; 1 omnibus book
Kathleen & Jimmy:		paint box and sketching block
Aunt Marie & Marion:	2/6d	

We played in the garden until bedtime at 8 p.m. Lights out is at 9 p.m. I have had a very jolly birthday but it was very much out of the ordinary.

28 June: I woke up very late and had to dash for washing. Breakfast was bread and marge as usual. We finished work early so we played in the garden until dinner time. For dinner we had fish cakes and haricot beans and semolina pudding. I am writing this in the garden. We are going to have a bath this afternoon. [later] We have had our baths so we played about, had tea of bread and jam and then read in the garden until supper (cocoa) at 8 p.m.

29 June, Saturday: This was a very dull day. Cornflakes for breakfast. Worked in the morning. Our system of working is this. I am on the second floor. Miss Mahy has charge of us and we do all the bedrooms and bathrooms on the floor. I am a sweeper. We had our identification cards given out today. I am NNA 135173. After dinner we played cards, games, etc. then we had a bread and butter tea. It has been a miserable day (the weather I mean).

30 June, Sunday: Got up at usual time. Cornflakes for breakfast and then we worked until dinner time. For dinner we had lamb (tough, I think it must have been mutton which had had its face lifted) and beans and potato, and sago pudding. At 2 p.m. we went to St Aidan's church for a special children's service. Our singing was awful but the vicar, Rev. Sockett, preached very well. For tea we had bread and jam and fruit cake (with stones by the thousand). We played games and then went to bed.

1 July: We had cornflakes for breakfast and then we had to go to school. The school is quite a distance from the house, about a mile. It is a council school we share (there wasn't any other school with available room). We have to go through a lane under a railway bridge, across a canal, past three factories and up a narrow street. School starts at 10 a.m. We arrived there at about the proper time and we were shown into our allotted classrooms. The head, Mr Wilson is very nice. We went back to Roylelands to dinner which was sausage and then ginger pudding. We went back to school in the afternoon. For tea we had bananas and bread and butter. We had indoor games and then cocoa supper (of course it rained, as usual). We as usual talked after lights out and had a bit of a feast with someone's tuck box.

Diana Falla (right) in Reading in 1941 with her sister Kathleen and nephew.

2 July: [This entry is headed Black Tuesday] Once a week we stay and do the housework at Roylelands and our turn was today. We had cornflakes for breakfast. At dinner time the bomb-shell came. Guernsey had been occupied on Sunday June 30th by the Germans. I was very glad I had not been to school as I heard there had been some very sad scenes. I was so dazed I did not cry. To take our minds off the news the staff arranged sports in the afternoon at the park with chocolate for prizes. I came second in the ball and spoon race. [In the] morning I received a lovely box of bars of chocolate from Mrs Payne. We had stew for dinner. Everyone was very kind to us. We had our tea and then went to bed in a very miserable state.

3 July: By this time we had cheered up a bit. I received a letter from Kathleen [Mrs Bain, her sister in Reading, Berkshire] telling me that from now on I had to think of 120 [Woodcote Road, Reading] as my home. I wrote to her before breakfast. We had apples for breakfast and then we went to school for 10 a.m. We came back at 12 and after a pie dinner and prunes went back at 2 p.m. I had a lovely surprise at school. Maurice [Wilson, a relative who was one of the Guernsey teachers who had evacuated with another school] came to see me. He told me that his mother is very worried. They get very much better food than we do. He very kindly gave me 5/6d for my birthday. I gave 3/- into the bank but I kept 2/6d for my immediate needs. For tea we had bread and jam and cake then after reading we went to bed. The girls at school seem very nice.

4 July: I felt pretty awful this morning but I managed to get to school but I felt so bad they took me back to Roylelands. I slept until dinner time but I did not eat anything. I read all the afternoon. For tea I ate tons of bread and lettuce and bread and jam. Now I am writing in bed and I feel quite OK.

5 July: I got up but had no breakfast. Went back to bed and had a miserable day. In bed all the time. Nothing happened except that my feet got very cold. I had a jolly good tea of bread and jam.

6 July, Saturday: I stayed in bed until 6 p.m. The doctor says I mustn't get up for more than an hour at a time. I think she thinks I've got tonsillitis. I had the usual bread and jam tea. I had my cocoa supper in bed. It is rather fun to be in bed just for a rest. It's bitterly cold.

7 July, Sunday: Had a bread and jam breakfast and got up for lunch. The dear doctor came to see me again this morning. She is très posh, especially her hats.

She is really very nice. For lunch we had lamb and then banana custard. In the afternoon we went to St Aidan's and after a short service with rotten singing we had a banana tea. We played games until a cocoa supper. Bed was at 7.30 today instead of 8. I suppose they wanted to get us out of the way.

Overleaf: The pages in Diana's diary on which she described Roylelands, one of the houses in Rochdale used as a reception centre.

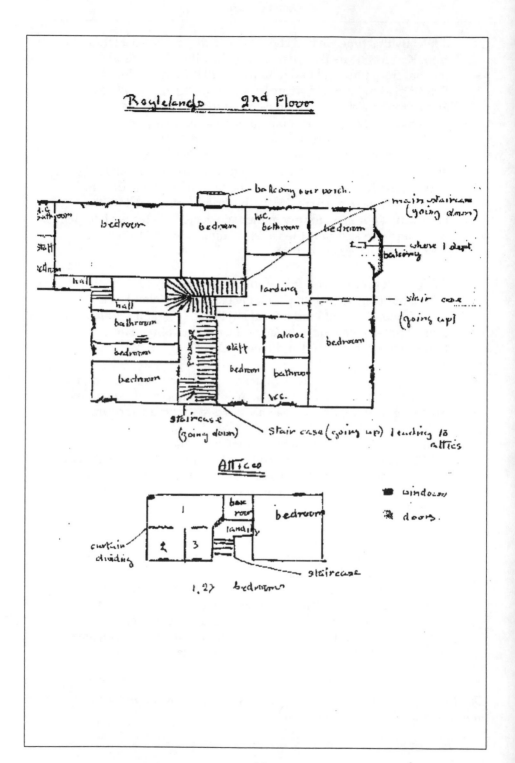

Roylelands   2nd Floor

balcony over porch.

main staircase
(going down)

a.c.
bathroom
bedroom   bedroom   w.c.
bathroom   bedroom   where I slept.
balcony

staff
bedroom

hall   landing   stair case
(going up)

hall

bathroom   passage   alcove   bedroom
bedroom   staff
bedroom   bedroom   bathroom
bedroom   w.c.

staircase
(going down)   stair case (going up) leading to
attics

Attics

bath   bedroom   window
room   doors.
curtain   landing
dividing   2   3
staircase

1. 2 > bedroom

84

Roylelands

It is a large house standing back from the road. The rooms are large and airy. The late owner was Mr K. Menzies so we found out. The staff had two bathrooms and so we had to queue for washing. The rooms took a lot of keeping clean we slept on beds borrowed from the ARP. They were allright at

first but schoolgirls are hard on beds and by the time I left most of them had a terrific sag in the middle.

The rose garden — s on the verge of colapse, and the vegeteble garden cos'nt it was just a mass of weeds. There were hardly any flowers only bushes and things. The lawn was quite nice.

When I were moved to an upstairs bedroom we used to go on the balcony untill Miss Roughton told us off. I think it was jolly mean of her. There were terrific fire places there

8 July: Miss Brittain said I must not go to school this morning so I did nothing after an apple breakfast. I received a lovely parcel from Kathleen. In it were two bars of chocolate and a sketching block. For dinner we had sausage and mash. We went to school [in the afternoon] and had singing with Mr Wilson, the headmaster. He thinks too much of his voice and playing. For tea we had lettuce as usual. We played games and had supper.

9 July: It was our day to do housework so we had to slave till a potato lunch. Miss Macfale(?) said as I had been ill I had better not work this afternoon so I started to sketch the view from the bedroom window. I have never washed or dried so many dishes in my life. Today we had two biscuits for supper as well as cocoa.

10 July: We got up at 7.30 and set off for school at 10 a.m. We had shepherd's pie for lunch and semolina pudding. Back to school. Tea, bread and jam and cake. There are some nice girls at school. Audrey Smith, Nellie, Janey, Mary and Doreen. In the evening we had extra green bits fitted to our gas masks.[she sketches the position of the 'extra bit']

11 July: It's a miserable day. I had some chocolate pinched. For dinner we had stew that tasted like dish water and ginger pudding. Then school again. It's perfectly horrible weather as usual. I get very cold feet at night. I think I shall develop pneumonia.

12 July: Breakfast we had cornflakes, then school. The other school is breaking up for a week, lucky beggars! For dinner we had fish cake, and lettuce for tea as usual. The girls [local girls from the school] came and played with us. Audrey Smith is tall with long, fair curly hair. She is very nice and pretty. Nellie is dark with glasses and little Janey is very funny (Ha! Ha!, I mean). She is small with freckles. They all have very broad Lancashire accents. They play with us in break.

13 July, Saturday: Cornflakes for breakfast and then housework for the remainder of the day. Stew and chocolate pudding for dinner. In the afternoon some of us set out for Roundley Moor. We caught a bus into town then we walked up to Horse Carrs (it looks very gloomy) and down the hill into a little village. Then up a hill and along a lane which ran by the side of a railway track. When we left the railway we went down a hill with cliffs on one side and a lovely river valley on the other. This led us into the grounds of a very old disused factory. We then crossed a narrow bridge and began to ascend a steep hill. On the way we met some of the Horse Carrs people [other evacuees]. We came to a piece of moorland...into a very quaint and dirty village. The scenery is very bare and rugged but rather beautiful. We then walked through the cobbled streets and down a long steep hill back to the town. It was a lovely walk but we were tired. We all ate enormous bread and jam teas. Rochdale is built in a curved valley and when we were near Horse Carrs we counted 31 factory chimneys.

14 July, Sunday: Cornflake breakfast and then work until the usual lamb, and custard and bananas dinner. I had a bath this afternoon just before going to church (We only get one per week). Today the Rev Sockett produced his own choir ladies so the singing bucked up considerably. But the giggling choir boys were simply awful. For tea we had fruit salad and cake. After this, being very energetic, I wrote a letter. We found out that Gracie Fields was born in a house in the main street. A postman supplied us with the information. The people up here are very kind to us.

13 July: Cornflakes for breakfast. For a change we had potato pie [dinner]. Of course we had bread and jam again for tea. What with the trains which run at the bottom of the garden and cold feet I get about five hours sleep.

16 July: Up at 7.30 and cornflakes for breakfast. I don't think I shall ever want to see cornflakes again. School as usual and beastly lessons. Dinner was shepherd's pie. Hazel Maplestone and I had to scrub out the wash house floor. I don't think it had been scrubbed for years. Millions of dishes as usual. Bread and jam and cake for tea, then more washing up, then supper, then more washing up. Then we laid the breakfast and got into bed dog-tired.

17 July: Cornflakes. School. Mrs Morgan took us for geometry. I'd like to ring [sic] her neck. For dinner we had potato pie and spotted dick.

18 July: CF (short for cornflakes). Miss Mallet says that Maurice is coming on Saturday to see about my going to Kathleen. For dinner we had stew then everything happened as usual.

20 July: Could hardly sleep for excitement. It's exactly a month today that we left Guernsey. Part housework for us today so we had to do some dishes. In spare moments I mended my stockings. Then I had my dinner (stew and ginger pudding), then Miss Mallet came and told me that we were going to have lunch in town. We went to a restaurant and had a terrific feed. I had never been in the town properly before. The menu was: Grapefruit, fish and chips, tart and cream, fancy cakes. (Oh boy what a feed). We wandered around town for a bit and then Maurice bought Miss Mallet and I a box of chocolates each. Then we went to the flics to see 'Remember.' It was quite nice. The other girls went to see 'The Other Thin Man.' Maurice is in Cheshire with his school.

21 July: Sunday. Worked in the morning. Had lamb as usual. A shop refrig broke down and so the ices wouldn't keep and the nice shop person sent them to us. It was good.

22 July: Lots of telegraphing went on about me. Miss Roughton [the head teacher] says I am to go to London with [blank space] and Jimmy [Dr. Bain] will meet me there. I went to the station with her this evening and she bought 10/- of my ticket (it was 14/-). I think it was jolly nice of her. I walked back and bought some chocolates on the way and we had a bean feast. Miss Clayton said she was very sorry I was going. I wasn't but I didn't tell her so. I forgot to mention that we have had a good many midnight feasts here.

23 July: Got up at 5 a.m. instead of 6 and did a jig-saw in waiting. [Caught] the 8.45 train. I bought a book on the station. We went to Manchester and had to change. Like a silly ass I dropped my book on to the railway line and it would have been lost forever but some kind person rescued it for me. It took us 5 hours to get from Manchester to London. We arrived at Euston and Jimmy was there to meet me.

Diana arrives at the home of Mrs Kathleen Bain in Reading, Berkshire. Kathleen is her 30-year old sister, married to Dr. Jim Bain, a local GP. They live at 120 Woodcote Road on the northern outskirts of Reading, Berkshire. Soon Diana joins a small private school in Reading. She writes nothing in the diary until Christmas and then begins to make daily entries again.

Her sister's home, a detached house close to the picturesque wooded countryside of Mapledurham and Kidmore End at the foot of the Chiltern Hills, was a pleasant place to live. Diana took pleasure in helping to look after Kathleen's baby, born a few weeks before she arrived. Diana was obviously stimulated by her new life. She often went on long country walks which she describes in the diary. She made frequent visits to the theatres and cinemas in Reading and sometimes went to London shopping with her sister. They also went to the monthly meeting of the Berkshire (later Reading) Channel Islands Society.

She rarely mentions her parents, who had remained in Guernsey, but when Red Cross messages began to arrive, she pasted them carefully in the diary and it is clear that the absence of any real news from Guernsey was like a dark cloud hanging over an otherwise happy time of her life. This was especially so when on 29 October 1941 Kathleen received a Red Cross message from Mr & Mrs Falla in Guernsey: 'Have sold Diana's bicycle and watch. Railway left us penniless.'

Mr Falla had been employed by Southern Railway.

These messages disturbed Diana but she did not seem to be worried by the bombing of Reading. On the afternoon of Wednesday, 10 February 1943, she is watching a film in the Central Cinema, Reading, when there is an air raid warning and almost immediately a bomb falls in an adjoining street, demolishing the Labour Hall, (where the CI Society have been holding their monthly meetings). That evening Diana described the street scenes in her diary with much detail, even drawing a sketch to show which buildings were damaged. '33 were killed,' she notes. 'Not much left of Minster Street.' Later she records that there were actually 50 fatalities.

She loves to meet other Guernsey people and always records chance meetings with any Channel Islander. In August 1943 she goes on holiday to a farm near Newquay, Cornwall. She enjoys her weeks there immensely but when she sees Fristal Bay the grey cloud descends again because, 'this part of Cornwall is so like Guernsey that it makes me more homesick than I have been for some time. Fristal Bay reminds me of Grande Rocque.' On the following day she goes to the Citizen's Advice Bureau in Newquay and asks for the address of the secretary of the local Channel Island Society. 'After a lot of bother it was produced.' but evidently it led to nothing for it is not mentioned again in the diary. However, that same afternoon (17 August) she sees someone from Guernsey whom she recognises. 'It was Mrs Noel, who used to teach us singing at Intermediate.'

Diana is overjoyed to find that Mrs Noel was with her daughter-in-law, Mrs Cecil Noel and her grand-daughter Nancy. 'I know the eldest daughter Pat Noel very well as she used to be in the same form as me.'

On 17 September 1942 Diana began to attend The Abbey School, Reading.

She does not seem to have kept a diary after October 1943 so nothing is known about her reactions when the Channel Islands were liberated in 1945, or when she returned to Guernsey. However she did not stay in the island for long. Soon after the war she was studying art at Reading University until 1949. Later she married Charles Nichol and continued to live in Reading. She died in January, 1979.

Channel Islanders at the offices of the Channel Islands Refugees Committee. The interviewer is Miss Le Pelley.

Chapter 7

The Refugees Committees

What has always been striking is the marked desire of the Islanders to stand on their own feet. They had a sturdy character and it took little time for those of them who could take up employment to become independent, self-supporting members of the community, and their first action was always to build up homes for themselves in this country. If I were able today to address my words to those left in the Islands, I should tell them that their fellow islanders over here have shown splendid resolution, facing the difficulties of their position with commendable determination to help in our war effort. Those we have over here are a splendid advertisement for the Island...

Ernest Brown, MP, in a speech on 4 December 1942, when he visited the offices of the Channel Islands Refugees Committee.

There were of course many Channel Islanders already settled in the UK, particularly in the London area, when the evacuation took place. In fact as early as 1896 a number of Jerseymen, mainly professional men such as lawyers, architects and civil servants, had formed The Jersey Society in London. By 1940 this had a membership of about 200 Jersey people and had become well-known in Jersey.

The chairman of the Society in June 1940 was Mr C.T. Le Quesne, KC. As soon as the Occupation had started and it was apparent that there were many distressed Channel Islands refugees Le Quesne and another prominent Jersey-man in London, Lord Justice du Parcq, called a meeting in Le Quesne's chambers of several Channel Islanders in London. This was attended by representatives of the Home Office and the Ministry of Health. About 30 people were present on the morning of Friday, 5 July 1940. A committee was chosen consisting of Lord Justice du Parcq, (Chairman) C.T. Le Quesne, (Vice-Chairman) G.D. Dillon (Auditor of States of Jersey) R.J.R. Farrow, (Ministry of Health) F. Geoghegan, (Auditor of the States of Guernsey), M.E. Weatherall, (Guernsey) H.W. Piper, (Alderney) H.W. Sayers, (Jersey) Ralph Renouf, (Jersey) and L.V. Bailhache. (A Jersey advocate who acted as Hon. Secretary).

This committee held its first meeting at 2 p.m. on the same day, and made rapid progress in obtaining premises, money and publicity. Du Parcq said later that they had no idea at first of "what the committee was to do or how it was to do it." They knew only that a great number of Channel Islands refugees would present many problems the precise nature of which could not be foreseen and there would be a real need for speedy and sympathetic assistance by a body of Channel Islanders. He said later, "I remember how ludicrously we under-estimated this need. We thought that if two members of the Committee spent a few hours each day at the office and answered the mail twice a week, that would be enough."

The accountant, Mr Geoghegan, offered the free use of his firm's premises at 67 Watling Street. Mr Farrow of the Ministry reported that the Maharajah of Gondal had presented a lakh of rupees (about £7,500) to the nation for the use of evacuated children and that the Ministry had allocated £1,000 of this for the use of Channel Island children.

The Committee issued a press release at once. The next morning the BBC announced the formation of the Committee in their news bulletins and within a few hours Channel Islanders were queuing at the Watling Street premises to ask for help. When Lord Justice du Parcq made one of his radio appeals in 1942 he described what one of the committee members remembered of that morning: "The day before we officially opened he went down to the office. When he turned the corner, he stopped dead. The street was full of people, in the main short, stocky people, standing in groups, talking as he'd often seen them at home. They were Channel Islanders: three hundred of them. He grabbed two of them whom he knew by the arm, took them into the office, and they spent the rest of the day registering the names and needs of the rest."

That evening C.T. Le Quesne wrote to one of the Home Office officials, Charles Markbreiter, 'We had a great rush today although the BBC did not announce the formation of the committee until this morning...It is plain that we shall need funds quickly... P.S. I was surprised how many turned up today. They sent an SOS to me and I went down to help.'

In the following weeks letters, many with donations, were delivered by the sack, far too many for the members to open, let alone answer. 50 volunteer helpers, many of whom were themselves CI refugees, were recruited and soon full-time staff were being employed. Gifts and donations of money poured in and to acknowledge and account for these was itself an enormous task. It was obvious that the premises in Watling Street were too small and by mid-July the committee had obtained the free use of premises at 34, Victoria Street, London S.W.

By the end of July the CIRC was being overwhelmed with requests for help. They were getting as many as 1,000 letters and personal enquiries every day. Much thought was given to the way they should organise their services. Four members, Weatherall, Sayers, Renouf and Falle prepared a report on which the future operations were based

On 30 July they received an offer from Lord Gray (Earl Gray) for the free use of 33, Eaton Place for the distribution of clothing. Major J.J.W. Evans had met du Parcq and had offered the service of the officers of the Royal Jersey Militia to give 'all the assistance in their power to CI refugees.'

The CIRC had no intention of being discriminatory when it helped Channel Islanders and Alderney people were given the same service as other islanders. But Judge French and other members of the States of Alderney who were in London decided that they would set up their own organisation which they called the Alderney Relief Committee. This eventually performed similar functions to those of the CIRC but it was not registered as a charity under the War Charities Act, 1940, so could not appeal to the public for funds. Their resources were therefore small in comparison with those of the CIRC but they were able to offer relief to a number of Alderney people from donations and grants given by the CIRC.

In January 1942 the CIRC member representing the Minister of Health, Mr R. Farrow, said that he thought confusion was caused by the fact that these two committees existed simultaneously and that from many points of view it would be a good thing if they could be fused into one body. However the Alderney members opposed any move to join with the CIRC. A small sub-committee of the CIRC and the ARC was formed and the outcome of their discussions was that the two committees worked separately but published their annual reports jointly in the same document.

In the last months of 1940 money poured in to the CIRC as a result of various appeals. By the end of the year the Committee had received £24,950, of which £7,285 was produced by a Broadcast Appeal made by Lord Justice du Parcq. Of this they had spent £1,344 on expenses (including £570 in salaries to staff) and they had given £14,118 to relieve hardship thus leaving a balance at the end of the year of £9,488. The average amount given for each hardship case was £10, the equivalent of about three weeks wages for a working man. Many of the grants were for furniture because it was recognised that this enabled families to move out of expensive furnished accommodation into much cheaper unfurnished rooms.

During the war the Channel Islands refugees fund came to be seen by the public as a major wartime charity. This was partly the result of several talks and appeals for money given on the BBC's Home Service by C.T. Le Quesne and Lord Justice du Parcq. A typical example of the way a collection for charity might be divided could be seen for example on 15 January 1944 when the *Brighton and Hove Herald*, reporting a meeting of the Patcham Women Conservatives, noted that they had collected £33 and divided this between the RAF Benevolent Fund, the Red Cross PoW Fund, the District Nursing Association and the Channel Islands Refugees Fund.

The CIRC set up several departments and as well as being involved with refugees also concerned themselves with the welfare of Channel Islanders in the Forces, especially prisoners of War and with the 2,000 people who had been deported in 1942 from the Channel Islands to camps in Germany.

The departments concerned with refugees in the UK were the Relief Department, the Clothing Department, and the Records Department.

Relief

The committee's aim was to try to make sure that the refugees did not feel friendless and destitute. They knew that thousands of the refugees had no relatives or friends who were settled in the UK and the members of the Committee saw their role to some extent as being a substitute for a close relative who could offer sympathy and practical help.

It was clear to the CIRC that their main task must be the relief of acute distress. Many of the refugees were mothers with young children who could not take a job. Others were too old or too infirm to earn a living. In these cases they could obtain, as could any other resident of the UK in similar circumstances, a small amount of money from what was then known as the Assistance Board (under the control of the Ministry of Health). But whereas a UK resident would have friends and relatives to turn to for other help, the CI refugee had no one to turn to and this meant being billeted and having a weekly income of 1/6d for an adult and 6d for a child.

Their final report laid stress on the financial help given by their Relief Department, which was headed by Mrs Houlgate assisted by Mrs E. Bois and Mrs E. Obbard. Their principal work:

> lay in paying doctor's bills, in providing help with convalescence, providing layettes and perambulators, paying for operations, looking after eyes and teeth, making advances in the case of sudden misfortune and helping with furniture grants.

Clothing

During the summer of 1940 it soon became apparent that most refugees would have inadequate clothing for the winter. This was particularly so in the case of the unaccompanied children in the northern counties. The CIRC decided in August 1940 to set a minimum standard for the amount of clothing which every Channel Islander should own and to take responsibility for seeing that the refugees were supplied with enough items to reach this. The standard for children was

> Macintosh, gum boots, warm suit or cloth frock, 2 sets of warm underclothing, 2 shirts, 2 pairs of socks or stockings, 1 pair of boots or shoes, Jersey or Cardigan, 2 sleeping suits, warm overcoat, sandshoes, ties, collars, handkerchiefs, toothbrushes, etc.

The Hon. Director M. E. Weatherall, wrote to the Town Clerks in the billeting areas in the north asking how many CI children were in their areas and saying that as the Ministry of Health would not be able to make provision for reclothing Channel Island children the CIRC would appeal for money to help. 'We were shocked to hear that some of our children were practically bare-footed,' wrote Mr Weatherall. 'If this is the case in your district please do let us know at once what sum of money you require to remedy the situation.'

Most of the replies said that winter clothing might be required later. The CIRC's minutes record on 23 September 1940 that the clothing position 'was still obscure.' On the one hand officials were saying that all was well but independent groups, including the children's teachers, were saying that the clothing situation was most unsatisfactory.

No immediate reply was received from Glasgow but a year later the Committee was astonished to receive from Glasgow Corporation what the chairman described as 'a formidable bill' of £2,900 for supplying clothing to Guernsey children. However by this time large donations were coming in from many different sources. They had recently received a letter from the Jersey philanthropist in South Africa, T.B. Davis, (1867-1942) offering £5,000 and Lord Justice du Parcq assured the Committee that part of this could be used to settle the bill from Glasgow. They were also getting donations from abroad, particularly from North America where, for example a 'Channel Island Aid Society' had been formed in London, Ontario and from the U.S.A. the American Guernsey Cattle Club offered help to the children of Guernsey cattle owners. A.W. Black of Montreal sent £1,000 and £262.10/- (250 guineas) were received from the British American Tobacco Company. Buckingham Palace donated £150 in October 1941, ('£100 being on account of the King and £50 on account of the Queen').

A clothing depot with WVS helpers.

By July 1941 Mr Weatherall was suggesing in the case of a particularly large offer that 'our balance sheet looked perhaps a shade too prosperous and it might be better to withhold this grant for the time being because experience seemed to show that it was much easier to get money for a charity with a very small bank balance than for one which, at a cursory glance, looked relatively flourishing.'

In addition to donations of money vast amounts of clothing were being received in late 1940 and by August 1941 Weatherall was reporting to the Committee that the estimated value of the clothing they had received was £20,000.

This came from various sources but much of it was allocated by the WVS from clothing sent by the American Red Cross.

Some Channel Islanders complained of feeling embarrassed when they were mistaken in the streets for affluent foreigners because they wore high quality items, often with gaudy colours, that had been sent from North America.

The distribution of clothing had presented the Committee with some difficult problems. During 1940 it was assumed that the WVS would distribute the clothing and in fact the WVS not only allocated substantial quantities from the overseas gifts but also bought clothing at wholesale prices, stored it and sorted out the required quantity for each child.

However the WVS tended to be too generous for Mr Weatherall's liking. Mindful of complaints that some refugees were getting more than a fair share of free clothing and that supplies might dry up he wanted to set up a system of investigating applications for clothing and recording issues. The ladies of the WVS did not like this, regarding it as unnecessary red tape.The CIRC minutes record the name of one lady, a Mrs Turner, who left a clothing depot abruptly, when she received a letter of instructions from the CIRC.

On 15 May 1941 the Committee received a complaint from the WVS about the distribution of clothing. Soon the dispute reached the highest level in the WVS and the formidable Lady Reading (1894-1971) met Mr Weatherall and Lord Justice du Parcq to discuss the matter.

Lady Reading was well known in government circles as a forceful, practicable and energetic idealist. In 1938 the home secretary, Sir Samuel Hoare, had invited her to set up a service of women who would give voluntary services to local authorities. The WVS, (the Women's Voluntary Service for Civil Defence) was the result and by the end of 1938 it already had 300,000 members. Its first major task was the preparation for the evacuation of 1 September 1939 when 1,250,000 children and mothers were evacuated from big cities.

After her meeting with Weatherall, Lady Reading told Lord Justice du Parcq that she wished to get two things done: the first of these was to get rid of Mr Weatherall and the second was to arrange for the government to take over the responsibility for clothing. In effect this meant that the WVS would be wholly responsible for clothing distribution because the voluntary organisation received a grant from the government and was regarded as a government agency.

The CIRC resisted both these suggestions strongly. They fully supported Mr

Weatherall. They were satisfied that the work of dealing with refugees was a most difficult task and they considered him to be most diligent and painstaking in the way he dealt with requests for clothing.

Waiting for help in the London office of the Channel Islands Refugees Committee.

In July the CIRC made a firm decision to take over sole responsibility for the clothing. Weatherall issued a carefully worded circular which began

> 1.   In the past the WVS have kindly helped the committee both in the provision and in the distribution of clothing to our refugees.
> 2.   My committee have felt that greater efficiency would be achieved were the responsibility for clothing CI refugees vested in one body. My committee have accordingly decided to assume this responsibility and in future they alone will undertake the clothing of Channel Islanders.

The circular then continued with details of how applicants should apply for clothing. The main clothing depots for Channel Islanders were in Chester and Halifax but there were smaller stores in Leeds, Bolton, Burnley, Manchester, St Helens, and Stockport. A refugee who needed clothing must now fill in an application form saying the 'number, size and type of garments required' and enclosing the relevant number of clothing coupons (A Clothing Rationing Scheme for the whole country had started on 2 June 1941). There had been cases of impostors who pretended to be Channel Islanders in need trying to get free clothing and the staff of the depots were instructed to send doubtful applications to the CIRC for verification.

It would have been impossible for the CIRC to run these and other clothing stores without the voluntary helpers who came forward wherever required and spent many hours sorting and issuing clothing. When news of the 1942 deportations to Germany came through, the CIRC knew that many of the relatives of those deported were refugees who could not afford to send parcels to the camps in Germany. The CIRC therefore took on the added task and many parcels of personal items and clothing, known as 'next-of-kin parcels' were packed and despatched by volunteers from the clothing store in Upper Grosvenor Street in London.

Throughout the war donations of clothing were received from a number of organisations, including the Canadian Red Cross, the British War Relief Society Inc. in the U.S.A., the Dudley House Allocation Committee and the Personal Service League.

Records

Many of the letters received by the CIRC in the first weeks were appeals for help from refugees who wanted to find relatives or friends who were also in the UK. In some cases whole families had been separated on arrival at Weymouth. In the summer of 1940 some children and parents were living with crowds of other refugees on the camp beds in large public buildings in the reception areas. They felt abandoned and the CIRC seemed to be their only hope.

The CIRC was quick to recognise that they should maintain records of individuals and at one of the first meetings they agreed to the expenditure of £25 on a second-hand card index system.

They decided to record the names and addresses of all the refugees in the UK and all who were known to have remained in the Channel Islands. By the end of 1940 there were five full-time workers dealing with enquiries and keeping records. The Ministry of Health supplied books with 14,000 names and British addresses of Channel Islanders. There were at least 50 letters of enquiry each day and some letters contained many enquiries. One enquirer from abroad sent a list of 127 names. This department was headed by Miss E. de Jersey and at the end of the war the Committee's final report noted that

> Miss de Jersey infused her staff with her own enthusiasm, and they followed every conceivable clue and developed an uncanny dexterity in the tracing of lost persons.

By 1945 the CIRC was able to report that it had a record of 'practically every refugee in Great Britain.' Months after the Liberation the Records Department continued to receive a heavy mail.

On Friday 4 December 1942 the CIRC was honoured by an official visit to their premises at 20, Upper Grosvenor Street by the Home Secretary, Herbert Morrison, and the Minister of Health, Ernest Brown. Both made warm speeches commending the work of the CIRC to which C.T. Le Quesne replied. The BBC six o'clock news bulletin carried a report of the visit with extracts from the speeches and the Home Secretary's encouraging remarks addressed to the people of the Channel Islands were heard by a few people in the islands and secretly noted in Leslie Sinel's diary entry in Jersey for the following day.

The bulk of the work of the CIRC involved financial help to refugees and the supply of clothing but the Committee never seemed inhibited about offering all kinds of help or encouragement to Channel Islanders, even those who were not refugees, such as servicemen, wherever they saw a need. They often acted more like a benevolent uncle than a bureaucratic organisation. When news reached them that several refugees had been killed or injured in a raid on Bath in 1942 Weatherall immediately sent a telegram to the Welfare secretary, Mrs N. Jean Adams, of the Bath Channel Islands Society:

> COMMITTEE SEND DEEPEST SYMPATHY TO ALL
> CHANNEL ISLAND SUFFERERS STOP PLEASE GO AHEAD
> MONEY RELIEF WITHOUT REFERENCE TO US STOP WIRE
> YOUR CLOTHING REQUIREMENTS TO ME STOP GOOD
> WISHES TO ALL WEATHERALL.

Knowing that all who were not in the islands were anxious to have any news they could get about conditions in their occupied homeland, the CIRC published reliable information whenever possible. British commandos brought back a bundle of Guernsey newspapers after a raid on Sark in 1942, and the CIRC went to the trouble and expense of studying these and publishing a 28-page booklet containing extracts from articles, advertisements and German orders.

The Committee also issued information warning Channel Islanders and their Societies about confidence tricksters. In March 1945 Weatherall wrote to all the CI Societies to warn them that

> ...several societies had been victimised by persons obtaining relief as Channel Islanders who were in fact not Channel Islanders. The Committee has a complete register of all Channel Islanders in Britain and can both quickly check up on any application and give aid if necessary....On 21 April 1944 a man described as well-spoken and plausible was charged at Merthyr Borough Quarter Sessions with obtaining money by false pretences. "He was convicted and sentenced to six months hard labour. He is now wanted at Chelmsford, Wallsend and South Shields for larceny. He usually describes himself as a Channel Islander and seeks out CI refugees and sometimes gets money from them.

The CIRC also helped with the financing of at least two meeting places for

Channel Islanders in London. One of these, known as Ma Cabine, was opened by an enthusiastic Jerseyman, George Vibert, at 27 Gideon Road, Battersea, on 24 May 1941. Here he provided cheap lodgings and meals for CI servicemen.

In the following year the CIRC agreed that a large room on the second floor of their premises at 20, Upper Grosvenor Street, London, W.1 could be used as a club for Channel Islanders. This became known as Le Coin and was a popular venue for social occasions until it closed in September 1945.

The Committee grasped at opportunities to foster CI unity. Early in 1945 the members co-operated with the BBC to organise a service of community hymn singing by CI refugees which was broadcast in in the programme Sunday Half-Hour on 11 March 1945. The last hymn on the programme was one which was said to have been adopted by Channel Islands refugees. Commonly known as the hymn for absent friends, it began,

> *Holy Father, in Thy Mercy*
> *Hear our anxious prayer;*
> *Keep our loved ones, now far distant*
> *'Neath Thy care**

The meeting at which it was decided to wind up the Committee was held on 14 December, 1945. Present were Lord du Parcq, Col W.H. Arnold, Gen Sir Beauvoir de Lisle, G. Dillon, M. Le Feuvre, and Weatherall, but the Committee met again 17 July 46 to consider the accounts.

During the war the CIRC distributed clothing to the value of about £500,000 to Channel Islanders and spent £80,456 on relief work. This money was raised from various sources but in particular from five appeals broadcast by the BBC in the Week's Good Cause programme. Results of these were:

1940	7,285
1941	3,505
1943	5,000
1944	7,300
1945	5,600
Total	£28,690

*Other verses in this hymn were reproduced on the membership card of the Rochdale CI Society. See illustration on page 102.

I have been home ill for four weeks and received National Health insurance and tickets for two weeks' bread, milk and groceries. I start work Monday but will not receive any wages the first week, a week being kept in hand, and no free tickets as I shall be working and they don't give any when off the sick list. Can you help me for one week? I have three children, ages, 13, 9, 3 and my husband is still in Guernsey.

One of many letters received by the CIRC .

ALDERNEY MINE

Island! Sweet island, I left far behind
In sorrow and anguish and pain,
No consolation, no friendship I find;
Oh that I could but remain.
Cities, how empty, have lost all appeal
To satisfy my aching heart.
Island of sunshine, my own aching land,
Why did we just have to part?
Alderney, dear, I'm longing for you,
Heaven's sweet isle of repose!
Dreaming of days idling there on your bays,
Soothed as the shadows they close;
Lulled into rapture my nature's caress,
Charmed by each flowered vine,
I yearn for your sunshine, your sweet solitude
Alderney, Alderney, mine.
I picture each pathway that winds o'er your cliffs
To meet golden sand far below;
Where waters they frolic and play with each rock
And flowered cliffs reflection they show.
The cry of the seabirds, the surf on the shore,
Still linger in sweet memory.
Loved ones and friendships all gone from me now,
Take me back to that isle of the sea.

Song written and composed by Henry Carlyle, Halifax
March 1943

HYMN FOR ABSENT FRIENDS.

Holy Father, in Thy mercy,
Hear our anxious prayer,
Keep our loved ones, now far distant
'Neath Thy care.

When in sorrow, when in danger,
When in loneliness,
In Thy love look down and comfort
Their distress.

May the joy of Thy salvation
Be their strength and stay;
May they love and may they praise Thee
Day by day.

Holy Spirit, let Thy teaching
Sanctify their life ;
Send Thy Grace, that they may conquer
In the strife.

Father, Son, and Holy ~~Ghosts~~ Spirit,
God the One in Three,
Bless them, guide them, save them, keep
them
Near to Thee.
Amen.

JERSEY	★	GUERNSEY

STOCKPORT and DISTRICT
CHANNEL ISLANDS SOCIETY.

FELLOWSHIP HOUSE, STOCKPORT.

Meetings : Weekly, Saturdays, 6-30 p.m.
Fortnightly, Sundays, 3 p.m.

ALDERNEY	Founded February 2nd, 1941	SARK

President :
HIS WORSHIP THE MAYOR OF STOCKPORT.
Vice-Presidents :
Professor H. J. FLEURE, Manchester University.
Mr. E. A. WEATHERALL, 34, Victoria Street, S.W. 1.
Chairman :
Mr. P. J. MARTEL, Queen's Road, Cheadle Hulme.
Vice-Chairman :
Mr. H. BRELSFORD, Red House Lane, Disley.
Treasurer :
Mrs. FINEY, 9, Woodfield Road, Cheadle Hulme.
Secretary and Registrar :
Mr. A. D. CREIGHTON, 82, Ravenoak Road,
Cheadle Hulme.

RULES.

1.—**Membership :** Open to all refugee Channel Islanders over school age. [Membership implies agreement with the objects of the Society and ready assistance in carrying them out].

2.—**Honorary Membership :** Channel Islanders and others introduced through the general committee.

3.—**Management :** The Society to be governed by a Chairman, Vice-Chairman, Treasurer, Secretary, and Committee, all elected annually.

4.—Members are expected to do all possible to advance the good name of their island.

COMMITTEE :

Mesdames Alexandre, Brelsford, Cripps, Creighton, Corbet, De Garis, De la Mare, James, Kimber, Marsden, Mollett and Reeves ; the Misses Proper and Squire.
Messrs. Duquemin, Lewis, Le Boutillier, Morley, Paul, Renier, Vidamour (J.), Vidamour (T.).

OBJECTS.

1.—To provide a centre of welcome and social fellowship for refugee Channel Islanders in Stockport and District.

2.—To keep active the spirit and influence of the Channel Islands.

3.—To encourage the collection and exchange of authentic (as far as can be ascertained) news of the Channel Islands and their refugees.

4.—To promote mutual aid and understanding.

5.—To establish contacts with similar societies and groups elsewhere.

6.—To stimulate a practical interest in the War effort.

Member's Name :

Typical membership card of a Channel Islands Society.

Chapter 8

The Smaller Societies

Unquestionably, the formation of this Society has had a tonic effect on the lives of the refugees in Stockport. The privilege of meeting together, talking of "home" and discussing news and views is indeed a valued one. So, too, is that of getting to know one another better and giving, wherever possible, sympathy and a helping-hand.

A. D. Creighton in the first issue of the Monthly Review of the Stockport & District Channel Islands Society, May, 1941.

By the end of 1940 many evacuees had found jobs and accommodation. Some had remained on the south coast, usually those with friends, relatives or enough money to rent accommodation in boarding houses and hotels in seaside towns. Soon there were several hundred Channel Islanders in Exeter and even more in the Southampton and Portsmouth areas. Some of those who had been sent to northern cities and towns found that they had only to travel a few miles south to reach more salubrious areas of cities in the Midlands. Leicester, Nottingham and Wolverhampton were popular with Channel Islanders. London too offered a vast range of job opportunities. Rented housing, furnished or unfurnished, was not difficult to find in any of these areas.

But it was mainly in the northern industrial towns that the refugees felt a stronger 'togetherness', perhaps because of their markedly different accents and vocabularies they felt more like foreigners than did refugees in the south. Ted Hamel tells how both he and his wife were embarrassed on different occasions because they did not realise that the word 'starved' in Bradford meant 'suffering from cold,' not 'very hungry.' In his workplace he was seen in a bad light by his northern colleagues because he addressed the senior men as 'Mister...' not realising that he should have used the Christian name. And in those days there were still many older Channel Islanders whose mother tongue was Norman-French and who could either speak little English or felt uncomfortable with it.

It is not surprising therefore that Channel Islanders began to meet together wherever they could and developed associations with a formal structure and regular meetings. In later years there was some dispute about which was the first but the strongest claim seems to have been by the Halifax Guernsey Society. This first recorded minutes of a meeting on 11 September 1940. 400 evacuees had arrived there at the end of June, nearly all from Guernsey. Ever since their arrival in Halifax one of the local councillors, Mrs P. Townend, JP, had taken a close interest in them and her name appeared on later correspondence as 'Founder and President' of the Society.

Another place where a Society formed soon after arrival in England was Leicester but although it was said to have started in August 1940 no documents confirming this seem to have survived. They called themselves 'The Leicester and District Society of Channel Islanders' and again a local councillor, Percy Russell, played a leading part in organising the Society and was elected their President. On several occasions the Lord Mayor of Leicester attended one of their functions. The society was active mainly in arranging social occasions such as whist drives, dances, and Christmas parties and outings for children. In 1941 a second CI society was set up in Leicester calling itself 'The Leicester Channel Islands Society.' This concerned itself more with welfare work and arranging meetings with talks and discussions.

It was not uncommon for there to be more than one Channel Island group in the same town. One would concern itself mainly with entertainments and the other mainly, but not exclusively, with serious meetings, gathering and distributing information and visiting other Channel Island groups. In Halifax there was not only the Guernsey Society but a few months later the Halifax Sarnia Club. This met for a monthly whist drive at the Auxiliary Fire Service Club in Hall Street. A news report about this club appeared on 1 October 1942 and records that, 'The first Tuesday in each month being the Guest Night, a Social and Dance took place at the Club Room in Hall Street, about 100 attending. Songs were given by Mrs R. Collins, Mrs M. Opie, Mrs Regan, Miss Greening and Mr F. A. Opie; monologues by Mr H. Carlyle; banjo duets by Miss H. Pidgeon and Mr H. Carlyle; also songs and recitations by junior members, finishing with dancing.'

In Scotland there were three societies in Glasgow catering for the needs and entertainment of Channel Islanders. The biggest was the Scottish Channel Island Society. The inaugural meeting was held in the hall of St John's Church, Glasgow where the Rev. J. Brazier Green presided and about 400 people attended. At that meeting Mr C.J.H. Rawlinson of Guernsey was elected President, and Mr A.C. Yourgis of Alderney as Vice-President. The Secretary was Miss E. Albiges.

This Society was one of the largest and most active in Britain. Meetings were sometimes attended by about 300 people. On one occasion they received a donation from a Canadian newspaper, the *Toronto Evening Telegram*, from which they financed a full day's entertainment for 600 Channel Island children. This was on Saturday, 23 January 1943 and included a morning showing of the Disney film Snow White at La Scala cinema. They were then taken to the Glasgow High School for lunch where they were addressed by King Peter II of Jugoslavia, who was introduced by the Lord Provost of Glasgow. Mrs Margaret Brehaut of Guernsey, an 8 year-old who was there on that day, told the author that one of her only memories now about her years in Glasgow was seeing 'a foreign King.'

Other CI societies in Scotland were the Glasgow Sarnia Fellowship Circle (later the Channel Islands Fellowship Circle) Secretary: Mrs Ruth Cann; the Channel Islands Knitting Circle – this was run by Mrs E. Le Friec and arranged a number of parties and entertainments for children but no record is available of the circle's knitted products; the Edinburgh and District Channel Islands Society.

Nearly all the 85 or so CI Societies which started and flourished during the war broke up in the weeks following the liberation in May 1945. People were unable to return at once to the islands but they were so excited at the prospect of going back, or of seeing their long-missed relatives and friends, that to many the Societies now seemed redundant, a stop gap that had served a purpose and would soon be forgotten. Few records have survived. A small number of Societies did continue to meet for several months after the war and some passed resolutions that they would establish themselves in their home islands.

The last meeting of the Slough and Windsor CI Society recorded in their book was on 29 July 1945 when there was much discussion as to whether they should disband as most members had returned to the CIs. Unable to agree, they decided to hold another meeting in September but there is no record of whether this was ever held.

The longest survivor is believed to be the Portsmouth CI Society. A card was printed in 1951 to announce its 10th anniversary. This read:

> This Society founded at a time of great distress to all Islanders and then continued after the liberation as a Social venture, takes pride in announcing its Tenth Anniversary and in wishing all old members and friends the Best of Good Luck in the future.. We still hold our Meeting monthly (except August) on the first Sunday and are always pleased to welcome old members or anyone interested in the Islands at The Masonic Hall, Albert Road, Cosham.

There is not the space here to record the variety of activities of all these CI groups (see Appendix A for a full list) but the following notes illustrate a little of the preoccupations of the CI exiles.

Federation

In 1941 some of the leading members of the CI Societies began to feel that it might be possible for all Channel Islands refugees to unite in some great movement which would not only be of benefit to them at a national level but would be a powerful voice when they eventually returned to the islands. By early 1942 almost all the CI Societies in the north of England had joined what they called the Northern Counties Federation. Mass meetings attended by hundreds, were arranged on 21, 22 and 23 February in Bradford, Bolton and Stockport. At Bolton where the Mayor presided, it was estimated that over 1,000 were present in Bolton's impressive Albert Hall.

One of the spokesmen for the Federation movement was the Revd. R.D. Moore. He travelled widely to give talks, sometimes with a strong political flavour, to numerous local CI Societies all over the country.

Moore encouraged his listeners to think about changing the Constitution of the islands after the war. His views were not always well received but 'Federation' as a topic stimulated much discussion about the future of the islands.

Victor Coysh, later to become a well-known Guernsey journalist, wrote in April 1942, 'let us not talk too glibly of CI representation at Westminster [after the war]. We have Home Rule—a privilege for which people have fought and died.'

When Diana Falla went to a meeting of the Berkshire CI Society on 19 April 1942 she noted in her diary, 'There were crowds of people there. A Mr Smith from High Wycombe gave an address. He is Jersey. They are always bringing up this federation. It wasn't frightfully interesting.'

That last sentence probably expressed the view of most islanders about forming a national movement . Federation was soon forgotten in 1945.

Freemasons

In 1941, Mr Fred W. Harris, an accountant and Guernseyman interested in Freemasonry, made strenuous efforts to form a new lodge primarily for Guernsey Freemasons. This was established as the Sarnia-Riduna Lodge on 17 October 1941 and still meets at Freemasons' Hall, London, W.C.2.

London

Evidently several prominent members of the old-established Jersey Society in London agreed privately that local CI societies were a useful and beneficial development. After the evacuation The JSL had opened its meetings in central London to all Channel Islanders but so many people had turned up that this proved an embarrassment. Sufficiently large meeting places could not be found with the result that the programme had to be run through twice on the same afternoon, and speakers were asked to give their talk to two different audiences. Dr Arthur Mourant, Philip de Veulle, H. W. Sayers and others therefore sent similarly worded private letters to CI people in their localities proposing the formation of a locally run society.

Dr Mourant lived in north London in 1942 where he was studying medicine. On 1 June 1942 he wrote to a number of Channel Islanders in his area proposing that they form a North London CI Society and suggesting that the objects would be:

1 To provide frequent opportunities for Islanders to meet;
2 To hold talks and discussions on subjects connected with the islands and on other matters of common interest;
3 Generally to promote a spirit of fellowship.

About 50 people attended the inaugural meeting on 9 June in the hall of the Presbyterian Church, Wood Green. Dr Mourant was elected Chairman and a Guernsey woman, Miss Maisie Gardner as Secretary. From then on meetings were held at frequent intervals throughout the war.

The other letters produced a similar result and within a few weeks there were active CI Societies in Hampstead, Kingston, Richmond, Croydon and other parts of suburban London.

Most tried to cater for a wide variety of tastes when they arranged their programmes. Activities for children were not neglected. We can get some idea of the enthusiasm put into these from a report written at the time by the North London secretary Miss Gardner about her Society's Christmas party in December 1942:

> About 70 adults and 40 children attended. It is rather necessary to enlarge upon the tea as it was most sumptuous. The tables were beautifully arranged...In the centre of the room was a low table with very low chairs where the youngest and smallest of the children sat. Here they did full justice to the tea, partaking of sandwiches, jellies and cakes. There was a variety of cakes but the most attractive to islanders was the Guernsey gâche and the Jersey wonders. Mr Ashton of Guernsey did the baking and his great masterpiece was the huge Christmas cake covered with chocolate icing. Dr. Mourant thanked all those whose efforts had gone to make the party a success.

In late 1942 and 1943 many new Channel Islands societies came into existence. Most were proud of their achievements and did what they could to get publicity by sending reports of their meetings to local newspapers and publishing annual reports. The sympathy and interest they received scarcely diminished as the war progressed. Looking through numerous reports one notices how frequently leading local citizens, usually the Lord Mayor or Mayor attended their meetings on special occasions. In Bolton the Mayor, Alderman Bleakley, made an official visit to a CI meeting and was reported to have said that, 'when peace returns the Channel Islands will be invaded by Lancashire holiday-makers, who, having heard so much of the islands, are now curious to see them for themselves.'

The *Dorset Daily Echo*, Weymouth, 26 Jan. 44, reported the annual meeting of the Weymouth & District CI Soc. Mr K. N. Denziloe said that the inaugural meeting in February 1943 was the most remarkable of the year when the attendance of 175 islanders and friends exceeded all expectations. The objects of the Society were:

1   To provide and foster social intercourse between islanders.
2   To circulate and pool items of news and interest contained in messages received from the islands, internees in Germany,

newspapers and other sources. The response of members to this had been excellent

3   To provide entertainment for members and children. During the year the committee had organised whist drives, dances and a concert and two treats for the children.

In Southampton the Mayor himself was a Channel Islander. This was Alderman R.J. Stranger, CBE, MC (1891-1976), a Guernseyman who had come to live in Southampton in 1919. He was elected President of the Southampton CI Society and took a close interest in the welfare of refugees throughout the war. Some of the evacuated Guernsey children remember their school being delayed before they boarded a ferry to return in 1945 while they listened to a Mr Stranger's farewell speech on behalf of Southampton Corporation. When Rex Stranger retired in 1970 he went to live in St. Brelade, Jersey.

By early 1944 there was a great spirit of optimism in the country that the war would soon end. When 300 members of the Bath CI Society met in the Pump Room in Bath on 13 May 1944 to see films of the Channel Islands the Mayor of Bath was there too and in his speech thanked the refugees for all they had done for the city of their adoption during their stay and he spoke of the 'great post-war possibilities of the islands as holiday resorts.'

Films of the Channel Islands were much in demand by the Societies and the secretary of the Jersey Society in London, Derek du Pré, began to borrow films and distribute them on request. The Southern Railway publicity department had made an advertising film of the islands just before the war and this was extremely popular. It was usually shown with amateur films from various sources. The audiences responded with much emotion when these films were shown and several newspaper reports refer to this. On 29 March 1941 du Pré wrote to a friend about a Society meeting in London at which CI films had been shown, 'it is a great sight to watch 325 Channel Islanders all (according to the Daily Mail) weeping heartily at films of their country.'

In Bath the films were arranged by Jack Knapman and when he sent one back to du Pré he wrote, 'The film was certainly appreciated…it was quite a moving experience to hear the warm applause at almost every scene and to listen to their comments afterwards.'

Other films were also shown. Diana Falla recorded in her diary for 15 November 1942, 'Went to a Guernsey meeting. They showed some very good films of Jersey, also some Charlie Chaplin films and one of Kew Gardens, but there was no news.'

Several CI societies received donations from unexpected sources. The Slough and Windsor CI Society was given £5 by King George VI in December 1943. In June 1943 the Sheffield and District Wholesale Fruit and Potato Merchants' Association gave £150 to the Sheffield CI Society and said, "We are a part and parcel of you. There is nothing to compare with CI produce. While you are in Sheffield we will look after you and see that you are never in want." In December

1942 the fruit and potato salesmen of Smithfield Market in Birmingham clubbed together to collect money for Channel Island refugees and were made 'associate members' of Birmingham CI Society.

The organisers of CI society meetings usually tried to create a nostalgic atmosphere at their meetings by having pictures of CI views on display. The Gosport Society went to considerable trouble to obtain old stocks of CI postcards from the pre-war publishers of postcards, Raphael Tuck, and these were on sale at their meeting. In Swindon the Methodist Church in Farringdon Road was decorated with ormer shells for a CI service on 20 June 1943, although how someone had managed to obtain such a large number of these shells is not recorded.

Well-known entertainers sometimes gave their service free of charge. One of these was Bruce Trent, a film star with a Jersey ancestry.

Most CI Societies were naturally in Lancashire and Yorkshire. By far the most influential of these was the Stockport and District CI Society.

Stockport is a large town about five miles south of Manchester city centre. Like other Lancashire towns it had a long history of textile production but it was particularly well known for felt-making and the manufacture of hats. On Sunday, 19 January 1941 the Stockport Rotarians invited a number of Channel Island refugees to 'meet each other in a social way.' Several of the islanders at this meeting decided to set up a formal group and two weeks later they met again, this time with 250 people present mostly from Guernsey but there were several from Jersey, and one woman, Mrs Gale, from Sark.

It was estimated at the time that there were 800 Channel Islanders in the borough of Stockport alone of which about 500 were adults.

The Stockport and District CI Society was founded that afternoon with a Guernsey school teacher, P. J. Martel, as chairman, another Guernseyman, A. D. Creighton as Secretary and a committee of fifteen.

The *Stockport Advertiser* reported the news on the following day:

> Folk who have long been separated from their homes and friends are always eager for news. Stockport's colony of Channel Islands refugees are no exception, and when they met in Fellowship House on Sunday afternoon, to form a Society, the most popular speakers were those who were able to give news of home, or of friends who are now scattered up and down the land.

Three sub-committees were formed: Entertainment, Information and Welfare. Soon there was a programme of regular whist drives, euchre drives, dances, etc. The Welfare committee at first worked in co-operation with the CIRC in London and helped to operate a local clothing store, although later disputes amongst its members resulted in a disruption to this work.

Within a few months the Society grew into one of the best known CI Societies in the country because in May 1941 the Information sub-committee began to publish a monthly news sheet. This began with four pages(135 x 210 mm) but the number of pages gradually increased until by the end of the war each issue had 24 pages. At first only a few hundred copies were printed as it was intended that it would circulate only to the members of the Stockport CI Society but it soon became a popular news medium for Channel Islanders in a wide area. It was published on the 12th of each month and sold at 4d. a copy or 2/- for a six-month postal subscription. It was sought after so much that back issues were reprinted and sold as bound volumes, each of six issues, at 1/7d each. For much of the war it had a print-run of over 5,000. In the last issue, dated July 1945, the editor, who by then was a former Guernsey newspaper man J. F. Le Pavoux, wrote, 'At its peak the Review had a net circulation of 8,500 and even that number was not sufficient to meet the demand, with the result that copies were often passed round for perusal. For instance one copy was sent by a mother to her son in India, then to a relative in Canada who in turn sent it to a relative in Australia.'

Some Societies were jealous of Stockport's success with their news sheet. When a delegation of Channel Islanders met in London on 18 July 1942 Mr Troy, representing the North of England Federation said that it felt very strongly that that the Stockport CI Society had no right to call their magazine *The Channel Islands Review*. The Federation thought it wrong that the control of the magazine should be in the hands of a committee which had no Jerseymen on it. There was loud applause when he said the papers should be in the hands of a committee elected by every Channel Islander in Britain. But most of the hundred or so delegates at the meeting fully supported the *Stockport Review*, including Dr Arthur Mourant who said he felt that all the CI refugees owed a tremendous debt to Stockport and to Mr Creighton, the editor for creating the Review which was now recognised by the government as being the official organ of Channel Islanders in Britain.

However there was a gap in publication between April and July 1942 because on 7 April the Ministry of Supply pointed out that under the Control of Paper Order 1941 it was unlawful to publish a 'newspaper, news bulletin, magazine or periodical' which had not been published before 16 August 1940.

Creighton and other members of the Stockport CI Society made vigorous appeals and asked the CI Refugees Committee for help. By May questions were being asked in Parliament and there were sympathetic comments in *The Times* and other newspapers. On 25 May Lord Portsea made a long and emotional speech in the House of Lords, emphasising that the Review was important to CI Servicemen because it brought them what little news was available about the Channel Islands. He was supported by several peers, including the Bishop of Winchester who said, "The great majority of the people in this country are most deeply concerned about the islanders. They deeply regret that their islands are under enemy occupation, and have the profoundest sympathy with those who have been evacuated to this country. It is just because we have such sympathy with them that we are most anxious that this little newspaper should continue its useful work. There are a number of small groups of Channel Islanders all over the country. They are partly held together by the existence of this paper and they are able to receive a certain amount of news which otherwise it would not be possible for them to obtain."

The Earl of Mansfield pointed out that only four tons of paper were needed to publish the Review and that vast quantities of paper were being used for the publication of children's comics, small trade papers and papers devoted to sport and games as well as books, many of which was the lowest form of sensational and pornographic literature.

In reply the Minister of Works and Buildings said that he hoped the matter would be cleared up satisfactorily by the end of the week but the Government wished to be satisfied that the Stockport CI Review is the best possible medium for its purpose.

It was a fitting compliment to Creighton and his assistants in Stockport that the Ministry soon agreed to allocate the paper they wanted. Creighton later wrote, 'The reaction of the British people to this unfortunate contretemps showed clearly and unmistakably that the Channel Islands have not been forgotten, and that the friendly welcome, so evident and spontaneous two years ago, has neither lessened or grown dim. This surely is a bright augury for the future which we shall do well to cherish and deserve.'

However the Stockport CI Society did not always run as smoothly as reports in its Review implied.

The Chairman, P.J. Martel sometimes disagreed strongly with the Secretary, Creighton and this with other disagreements among the leading members seriously disrupted the activities of the Society. This friction became so bad that on 14 May 1942 the CIRC decided not to use the Society's Welfare Sub-Committee but to set up a new relief committee in the borough to act on their behalf. After reading comments and correspondence from Stockport Lord Justice du Parcq said the Stockport & District CI Society appeared to be 'split into several camps all of which are quarrelling violently with each other. The Chairman, Mr Martel, has broken off diplomatic relations with the Secretary, Mr Creighton, and Mr Creighton again was on no sort of terms with the present members of the Welfare committee.'

In the south

Another local CI society which became well-known during the war, but for quite different reasons, was the Gosport society. Gosport is a small naval town adjoining Portsmouth on the south coast. One of the refugees who lived there was a Jerseyman, Ronald Renouf. He believed that Channel Islanders should make every effort to raise money so that in some way food could be sent to the Channel Islands. With another Jerseyman in Gosport, David Dumosch, he called a meeting of Channel Islanders on 27 June 1943 and the Society was formed on that day. Renouf was elected chairman and Eric Brook, also from Jersey, became Secretary. Almost all the other members of the committee were Jersey people but there was a woman from Alderney, Mrs. F. de la Mare. Guernsey was represented by two young sisters, Miriam and Joan Richer, both in their teens.

It soon became clear that Renouf considered the main function of the Society should be to raise money and organise help for the occupied islands. The other members tried to guide the Society into simpler and local activities, telling him that 'it was too early to tackle a question of that magnitude.'

They arranged regular monthly meetings and by the end of the year had enrolled 80 members. The usual sort of social functions, whist drives, dances, children's parties, were held. Ideas were put forward for raising money. One of these was to obtain permission to use the Patience Strong verses about the Channel Islands which they had seen in the *Daily Mirror* and to publish a Christmas card. They raised enough money to enable them to have 1,500 printed in November 1943. The card was a remarkable success. More were printed and by mid-December they had sold 5,000. The profit was £57.

> *God scattered a handful of gems in the sea*
> *The islands where men were once happy and free*
> *Loyal were the people and fair was the land*
> *Now in the grip of an enemy hand*
> *Weep for their sorrows*
> *Remember and pray*
> *For the bright dawn of that glorious day*
> *When once again there'll be singing and smiles*
> *And you will return to the beautiful isles.*
>
> Patience Strong

By this time Ronald Renouf had realised that most of the members of the Gosport CI Society were against his 'Food Campaign' but he persuaded Eric Brook and David Dumosch to join with him in starting an organisation which they decided to call The Channel Islands (Enemy Occupied) War Relief Association. Renouf set his mind on launching this at what he called a 'mass meeting.' He had become friendly with the Jersey peer, Lord Portsea (Bertram Falle, 1865-1948), well-known for his long-winded speeches criticising the government for what he considered its unhelpful attitude towards the Channel Islands. On one occasion a Minister in the Lords had accused Lord Portsea of 'not helping our fellow subjects in the Norman Islands by hysterical misstatements' in Parliament.

Renouf and his friends after some difficulty managed to hire a large hall in Fareham, a small town to the north of Gosport. They advertised their new association and the 'mass meeting' heavily in local newspapers as far away as Somerset and Wiltshire. It was eventually held on 11 December 1943 and less than 100 people were present with hardly anybody from Gosport itself. The

President of the Portsmouth CI Society, Mr A. Conway, turned up with the sole intention of disrupting the meeting because he disagreed so strongly with Renouf's speeches against the government and his scheme to send a ship to the Channel Islands. His interruptions were described later by Renouf as 'an unruly outburst' and he later went to a meeting of the Portsmouth CI Society to protest about Conway's behaviour.

Despite the fact that Renouf's War Relief Association received almost no support from neighbouring CI Societies he and his friends persevered throughout 1944 with their efforts to raise money for their 'Food Campaign.' They received some help from a Scottish group called the Edinburgh CI Restoration Fund and they recruited a lady from an old Jersey family, Miss E. Malet de Carteret, who agreed to act as their national appeal secretary with an office in London.

The Horsforth CI Society in Leeds agreed to hold a flag day in the city and told Renouf that if it went well it would raise as much as £1,000. Renouf decided to help so he travelled to Leeds and spent three weeks there. The flag day raised £270, which was a substantial sum for a small organisation but by this time Renouf was talking about the fund's goal being £100,000 so he was disappointed that his weeks in Leeds had such a relatively small result.

But the worst blow came early in 1945. The Red Cross ship *Vega*, sailing from Lisbon, had delivered food parcels to the Channel Islands for the whole population. Every CI refugee was delighted with this good news and the Gosport CI Society persuaded Renouf's Association to offer their Fund to the Red Cross Society in the UK. Much to Renouf's dismay this offer was rejected by the Red Cross who suggested to the members that they should conserve this money for their needs when they returned to the islands after the liberation.

The Newquay Channel Islands Society.

Soon after the Liberation a committee was formed in Jersey and with Mr G. D. Smith as Chairman and working from an office in West's arcade (now demolished) in Peter Street the Committee announced that it would use its funds 'to assist those inhabitants of the Channel Islands who have suffered, whether by threat of Occupation, or from the occupation itself.' A similar announcement was made in Guernsey where an office was obtained at a café in St Peter Port.

The last words on the misguided but well-meaning efforts of the War Relief Association are in a letter from Dr Arthur Mourant dated 5 July 1945 written to the secretary of the Société Jersiaise:

> With regard to the CI Societies...we have only collected a small fraction of the masses of leaflets and similar literature which they have issued. One body in particular which I have not approached is the CI War Relief Association which has been a copious publisher of appeals, semi-political literature and lurid accounts of life in the islands. I had intended to ask them to send their literature for historical purposes, making it clear that my committee did not associate itself in any way with its propagandist activities.

Rochdale and District

Patron - - - THE RT. HON. LORD PORTSEA	*Chairman* - - - - MR. H. F. FARAMUS
President - - HIS WORSHIP THE MAYOR OF ROCHDALE	*Vice-Chairman* - - - MR. F. G. THOMAS
Vice-Presidents - THE MAYORESS OF ROCHDALE GEOFFREY DUCKWORTH, ESQ. and MRS. DUCKWORTH.	*Treasurer* - - - - MR. R. A. COX
	Secretary - - - - MRS. D. M. COOPER 5 St. Albans Street ROCHDALE, Lancs.

Society

FOUNDED 30TH NOVEMBER, 1941

Letterhead of Rochdale and District Channel Islands Society.

Chapter 9

The Red Cross Messages

I had many things to write, but I will not with ink and pen write unto thee: But I trust I shall shortly see thee, and we shall speak face to face. Peace be to thee. Our friends salute thee. Greet the friends by name.

from The Third Epistle of John, 13,14
Text mentioned in a Red Cross message from
Mr & Mrs N. W. Mahy, Sandland, L'Islet, Guernsey
and received in Lancashire 12 August 1942.

For many evacuees one of the most painful experiences of their exile was the anxiety caused by the lack of information about the welfare of their relatives and friends in the islands. This worry was worsened by alarming newspaper reports and rumours. In August 1940 the *Sunday Dispatch* published an article purporting to come from a man who had escaped from Guernsey to the effect that all women were being placed in concentration camps and the population was already near to starvation. The editor, when asked by officials at the Home Office, refused to reveal his source. This article caused much distress to many evacuees. As the war progressed headlines such as the following were not uncommon.

CHANNEL ISLANDERS EATING POTATO PEELINGS
(*Portsmouth Evening News*, 13 December, 1943)

HUNS WHIP SLAVES TO DEATH ON BRITISH SOIL
(*Daily Mirror* 23 February, 1944)

STARVATION DIET IN DISEASE-RIDDEN CHANNEL ISLANDS
(*Leicester Mail* 4 December, 1944)

Few evacuees could have imagined in that hectic summer of 1940 that such a solid wall of silence would come between them and their homeland. Even the British government in the early years of the war had no information on what was happening in the islands.

Prisoners of War were protected by an international convention which allowed them to send letters but civilians in occupied countries had no legal way of communicating with the outside world until the International Red Cross developed a scheme which started in December 1939 by which twenty words of family news could be sent to a relative. At first this scheme operated only from the United Kingdom to Germany, Austria, Czechoslovakia and German-occupied Poland but as more countries were occupied it was gradually extended and the Channel Islands were included from December 1940. The permitted number of words was later increased from 20 to 25.

By early 1941 a few messages were arriving in the UK from Jersey and Guernsey in response to Red Cross enquiries. On 18 January 1941 the Channel Islands Refugees Committee prepared a leaflet in which they tried to answer some of the many questions which were being put to them. This included a statement about enquiries through the Red Cross but pointed out that no replies had yet been received. A letter dated 20 August 1940 had been received in the UK from Guernsey via the British Vice-Consul in Lisbon.

The secretary of the Jersey Society in London, on hearing rumours that messages were coming in, wrote to the British Red Cross Society on 14 April 1941 to ask for information. Mrs I. J. Mills of the Foreign Relations Department, told him that about five hundred very short messages had been received in answer to Red Cross lists of names and addresses sent in August 1940. 'The general tenor of the messages is cheerful,' wrote Mrs Mills. 'All are dated between the last week of December 1940 and the first half of January 1941. We gather that food, though strictly rationed, is not scarce; the Germans appear to be behaving with considerable discretion, and not interfering with the civilian population.'

Any information at all from the Channel Islands was considered a newsworthy event even by the national papers. On 20 May 1941, *The Daily Telegraph* published a letter from W. A. J. Blampied, saying that he was 'the fortunate receiver of two messages from my folk in Jersey, the first since the invasion. One message from my brother contains news which tends to assure us that the normal life of the island is being maintained...This information may help to reassure others...'

The People reported under a headline CHEERFUL IN THE CHANNEL ISLES on 25 May that messages had been received.

In fact Mrs Mills of the Red Cross had written to Derek du Pré on 22 May to say that since her earlier letter thousands of messages had been received and 'we expect a steady flow of answers from the islands. The approximate time these messages take appears to be between four and five months from the date the message is despatched until a reply is received.'

To send a message you had to go to a Red Cross Bureau (this was usually attached to a Citizens' Advice Bureau) and write your message in not more than 25 words on one of the Red Cross forms. On both sides of the Channel some people put considerable thought into condensing as much information as they could into so few words. Nan Le Ruez in Jersey noted in her diary entry for 9 April 1942: 'Wrote out the answers to our Red Cross messages. It takes quite a time to concoct these messages of only 25 words.'

As we shall see later in this chapter a few were ingenious in their attempts to conceal a hidden message within an apparently ordinary statement of family news.

The route of the messages was so circuitous, both to and from the CIs, that it is not surprising that they took several months to arrive at their destinations.

The local Red Cross Bureau sent the forms to the Red Cross Headquarters in London. They were then sent to the G.P.O. for censoring before being taken by sea to Portugal. From Lisbon they went either by train or by sea (via Marseilles) to Geneva where they were inspected by officials of the International Red Cross and stamped with a cachet before being sent to the German Red Cross in Berlin. From Germany they went to Paris where there was more censoring, this time by the Germans. When they finally arrived in Jersey and Guernsey they brought a brief comfort and joy to many. Nan Le Ruez received two from her fiancé on 13 February 1941 and took them to show to her friends. That evening her diary entry was, 'What a difference this bit of news has made to us all we are full of new hope and courage now and don't feel so dreadfully cut off.'

Although the messages received by the refugees were entirely personal, (the instruction on the printed enquiry form was 'not over 25 words, family news of strictly personal character') they were not treated as being private. When Mrs Mills wrote to the Jersey Society in London she enclosed extracts from what she considered the more interesting and revealing messages. These were read out at meetings and people who had received messages often handed them round for others to read, or they read them out aloud to the meeting.

As soon as these first messages were received, The Channel Islands Review published long reports containing the names of the recipients and summarising the news they had received. Within a few months this was a major part of the news sheet and it often had several pages containing the complete text of messages.

Many messages could not be delivered. Mrs Mills wrote to the Jersey Society in London on 23 July 1941, 'We have experienced a great deal of trouble in forwarding replies to people who have not notified us of their change of address since making their original enquiries and I wonder whether you can help us in any way.' Typewritten lists of 10 pages of names and addresses were enclosed with this and with subsequent letters when a few weeks later messages which had been originated in the Channel Islands began to arrive in thousands, many with inadequate addresses.

By the end of 1941 the Germans were allowing islanders to send one message each month so the Red Cross offices in England had a major task of distribution. Their long lists of unclaimed messages were sent to county police forces and Citizen's Advice Bureaux.

On 18 July 1942 complaints were raised at the Channel Islands conference in London because restrictions were being placed by Citizens' Advice Bureaux on the number of messages which could be sent. In some places refugees were allowed to send only one message a month but in others there was no limit and it was said that there was one man who regularly sent about a hundred a month. Some delegates complained because refugees were not permitted by some Bureaux to sign the message forms themselves. In reply it was said that it depended on how busy a local bureau was. If they were not under pressure they typed the message while the sender waited, and then it was signed. But some Bureaux asked the sender to sign a piece of adhesive paper and this was later stuck on a Red Cross form when the message was typed by staff at the bureau. In Glasgow refugees signed blank forms on which the message was typed later.

The messages today

Many of the original message forms have been preserved in family archives and are today much sought after by some philatelists. Detailed studies of the postal histories and markings on the forms have been made. The first book on the subject was published in 1975 and in 1992 David Gurney's comprehensive publication appeared. This contains a large number of facsimile reproductions of the messages themselves and the numerous cachets and postal marks which they accumulated on their long journeys as well as the official forms and correspondence relating to the service. For enthusiasts there is a lively world-wide market for all these items. Prices fluctuate. There are two basic Red Cross message forms: those printed in the UK and used by the refugees to send messages to the CIs; others printed by the Germans which were used by Channel Islanders. Good specimens of these now fetch around £4 at auctions but a rare marking can increase the value substantially. Correspondence from Red Cross sources relating to the message service is also likely to have a commercial value.

News from Mrs Hubbard

The arrival of messages was as comforting to the refugees as it was to their folk still in the islands, but in a different way. Many imagined that their relatives would be facing horrific experiences as a result of German brutality or at the very least suffering from severe deprivation of food and other essentials. It was therefore a little surprising to receive so many messages which seemed optimistic. When Mrs Mills wrote to the JSL on 22 May 1941 she quoted several messages to illustrate that most were 'of a very cheerful character.'

'Kindly allowed our wireless.' (Jersey)

'Jersey Ladies College thriving. Miss Christine Holt in charge as headmistress, Miss Barton had cycling accident.' (Jersey)

Nevertheless some people were suspicious, wondering whether islanders were being forced by the Germans to paint a rosy picture.

Philip de Veulle wrote to Kenneth Renault, then in Cheltenham, on 27 August 1941 saying,

A large number of messages have been received through the Red Cross. They are mostly of the 'all very well' type, but as far as one can read between the lines things do not seem too bad…One wonders, however, whether any other kind of message would be allowed to come through. Apart from these messages there is no reliable information as to what is happening.

Another reflection of the suspicion surrounding the early messages is that when notification of a death in the islands was received the words 'from natural causes' were sometimes added in the published version to reassure readers that there was no evidence of suspicious circumstances arising from the enemy occupation.

Messages were scrutinised carefully by the recipients. Early in October 1941 Mrs G. A. Marquis told the editor of the Stockport Review that at the top of her message the letters RCB, Guernsey, were typed, and from this it was correctly assumed that a Red Cross Bureau had been set up in the island.

As the months passed people began to notice more and more coded remarks in their messages. Many of these referred to Mrs Hubbard and as the recipients knew no-one of that name except the famous lady with an empty cupboard they assumed it was an allusion to a lack of food. It is remarkable that the censors on the German side did not smell a rat when they saw so many comments about poor Mrs Hubbard.

Some messages scarcely concealed their meaning:

'Ma Hubbard pretty bare. Are limpeting daily,' from T. Keyho, Guernsey, received September, 1942.

'Mrs Hubbard very low,' received by Mrs E.C. Bush from her brother, September 1942. A Jersey family who had a message which included, 'Food like Miss Wilson's' knew that Miss Wilson had been the owner of Jersey's Animals' shelter so this was taken to mean that 'our food only suitable for animals.'

There were many hidden comments letting people in the UK know that the Germans had forbidden people to listen to the BBC. One of the most succinct was:

'Miss Ben. No news George, Elizabeth,' from Tom Guilbert to his sister G. Guilbert of Alderney in November 1942. It was of course a reference to Big Ben and the King and Queen, and Tom's sister correctly interpreted it.

When Mrs K. B. Seaton had a message that 'Little Pye dead, very sad' she knew this referred to her mother's wireless, and knowing that her sister's radio was a Murphy she was not surprised to get a message that, 'Work very dull without Mrs Murphy.'

Sometimes however a message confirmed that certain radio programmes had been heard. Mr R.G. Harwood had a message from a friend in Guernsey dated 25 April 1942, It included, 'Heard from Banks, Friday.' He knew this meant that

Overleaf: A typical Red Cross message form. This one has a neat hole cut by a German censor to remove four words.

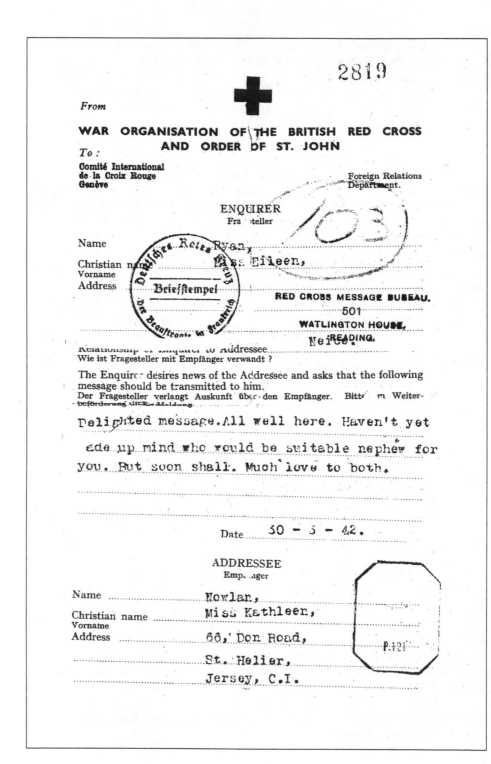

2819

From

WAR ORGANISATION OF THE BRITISH RED CROSS
AND ORDER OF ST. JOHN

To :

Comité International
de la Croix Rouge
Genève

Foreign Relations
Department.

ENQUIRER
Fra   teller

Name   Ryan,

Christian name   Miss Eileen,
Vorname

Address   RED CROSS MESSAGE BUREAU.
                                                    501
                                           WATLINGTON HOUSE,
                                           READING.

Relationship of Enquirer to Addressee.
Wie ist Fragesteller mit Empfänger verwandt ?

The Enquirer desires news of the Addressee and asks that the following
message should be transmitted to him.
Der Fragesteller verlangt Auskunft über den Empfänger. Bitte m Weiter-
beförderung dieser Meldung.

Delighted message. All well here. Haven't yet

made up mind who would be suitable nephew for

you. But soon shall. Much love to both.

Date   30 - 5 - 42.

ADDRESSEE
Emp   nger

Name   Nowlan,

Christian name   Miss Kathleen,
Vorname

Address   66, Don Road,

                        St. Helier,

                        Jersey, C.I.

120

March message received.   Am extremely

curious.   Suit yourself old dear, not me.

Both well and busy.

Heard from Phil.   Love. Chum.

27.5.42.

On behalf of the Bailiff
of Jersey's Enquiry and
News Service.

5 AOUT 1942

a BBC broadcast by Sir Donald Banks, a well-known Guernseyman in London, had been heard.

Mrs Betty Rees knew in October 1942 when she had a message from her uncle, Charles Hilliker, in Jersey 'Often hear from Jack Warner,' that he was listening to the BBC. Mrs H. Cartwright's message from her brothers in Guernsey in April 1942 included the sentence, 'Hear from Ben daily.'

Not only radios but vehicles were often commandeered by the Germans. This news too was easily hidden in short messages.

Arthur Tostevin had a message in October 1942 from Mr H. W. Bond in Guernsey which included 'See Stan Grey occasionally,' and as he knew no-one of that name but remembered that Mr Bond owned a grey Standard car, the message clearly meant that the car was being used by the Germans. Mr G. Carre also wrote to him at about the same time saying that 'Mr Austin gone.'

A more contrived message was received by Mr J.E. Baker from his sister in Guernsey in November 1942: 'Miss Sett and Mr Karswent evacuated.' As none of his family owned a car Mr Baker took this to mean that the Germans had confiscated cars as well as radios.

In December 1942 Victor Coysh reported that he had a message from his cousin Jessie Marriette 'Morris left us' by which he knew that her car had been taken.

Sometimes a message revealed far more information about a local matter than a censor could have suspected. Joss Higginbotham, a photographer at Jersey's *Evening Post* wrote to a colleague, R.F. Le Sueur, 'All fine here. Still working upstairs only.'

Le Sueur knew that 'upstairs' was where the half-tone blocks were made for the newspaper and if Higginbotham was only there it meant he was not able to take photographs outside. The message also revealed that the *Evening Post* was still being published.

Mr E.B. Best had a message dated 2 September 1941 from the foreman at St. Andrew's brickyard in Guernsey which told him that the stone quarry was still working. From this Guernsey people in the UK knew that the public electricity supply was still available because Mr Best knew that the crane and pumps could only work from electricity.

Much information was conveyed by naming people who were in certain jobs. When someone had a message from Guernsey saying that Thomas Keyho 'still doing the same job on cycle,' they knew that at least some of the Guernsey schools were open because Mr Keyho was the school attendance officer. From Jersey Mrs Peggy Tanguy had a message in March 1942 from the well-known musician Douglas Tanguy, 'Playing at Corner House nightly.' He had a dance-band so this was an indication that dances were being held.

From Jersey, Mr Charles Saunders, manager of the large Ommaroo Hotel, wrote in March 1942 to H. Lane saying 'Hotel flourishing' and naming several of the staff, so it was clear that life went on, although the recipient of the message could not have known that most, if not all, of the guests were German soldiers.

In time certain names became commonly used as code words in the messages and the Channel Islands Refugees Committee even recorded this in their minutes and explained them to strangers.

One of the Guernsey members had received a message in June 1942 which read, 'Nothing of Dumpers, Allens, Hydes or Ceylon. 18 months nothing of Sheriffs, Butts or Newcastle, very little Powells and Snooks.'

These were of course mostly Guernsey shop names. Dumpers meant cakes; Sherriffs meant drapers; Butts meant shoes; Newcastle was coal; Powells was meat; Snooks was bread; Allens was sweets; Hydes was fish and Ceylon meant tea.

Other shop names were mentioned in a message (sent from Guernsey 19 April, received in Yorkshire 19 July 1943) from J. Hubert to Miss L. Renouf: 'Never visit Burton, Creasey, Lihoy. Mr Bird never calls.' This was taken to mean that they could not get new clothing, tea or coal.

But there was sometimes good news concealed in a message. In one, written on 27 December 1941, the writer said, 'Xmas dinner, usual menu. Even Millie cfrtb.' The recipient knew this was a family abbreviation for 'crammed full, ready to burst.'

It was frustrating when some messages had words deleted or cut out by the censor. What was Mrs W. Trowbridge to make of a message dated 9 February 1942 from the organist at Brock Road Church, C.N. Falla, which read, 'All well home and Brock Road. Favourite hymn now [name cut by censor].' Today's reader may like to speculate on which hymn this was. Perhaps it was the one by Henry Burton which begins, 'There's a light upon the mountains,...' This continues with

> ...and the day is at the spring
> When our eyes shall see the beauty of the glory of the King.

When Eric Douglas received a message in December 1942 from Tim Ford who was in Guernsey it began 'Kitten stolen. Pigs eaten. Rabbits multiplying. Garden fruitifying...' The next ten words had been blacked out by the German censor.

However one wonders whether the censor looked up and approved the text mentioned in a message from N. W. Mahy of Guernsey who suggested on 12 August 1942 that she read v 13-14 of the 3rd Epistle of John.

The censor also missed 'Longing for Chorus 2' in a message written in the summer of 1942 by the parents of Clifford Tostevin of Guernsey. Mr and Mrs Tostevin were referring to a verse in a Salvation Army hymn which began, 'Bread of heaven feed me, till I want no more.'

Sometimes messages tried to convey information about German fortifications. On 31 July 1943 Mr J.M. Belford, a well known tobacconist of Jersey who lived at Sea Court on the sea front at Bel Royal wrote to his daughter Mrs Joy Thacker, 'Have to use plank and ladder for bathing, very inconvenient. Business very quiet.' She knew that his garden led directly to the beach so this told her that there were fortifications lining St. Aubin's Bay.

From Jersey a farmer of St Lawrence indicated in October 1942 the presence of enemy artillery by including in a message that 'Mr G. Cannon living in nearby field.'

A knowledge of Channel Island history helped Mrs H.O. Hubert to understand what her son Frank meant when he wrote in June 1942, "Had experience like Stella." Stella was the name of a passenger steamer which had struck a rock in fog on 30 April 1899 with the loss of many lives. In fact a German ship had struck a rock in fog off Grosnez on 5 May 1942 and several Guernseymen and the German crew had managed to scramble ashore.

Sometimes it was simply the way a message was written that told his relatives that the writer was keeping his spirits up. An example is a message in verse written by Charles H. Toms to his brother F.W. Toms on 8 April 1944:

> *Once again I plant and sow,*
> *Although I am a printer.*
> *The garden makes a good show,*
> *And feeds us through the winter.*

Senders of messages found no difficulty in referring to the Germans in an indirect way. Usually the familiar word 'Jerry' was converted to 'Gerald' so that messages like 'Gerald now living in your house' told a refugee that his house had been taken by the military. This does not say much for the alertness of the German censors who were instructed to delete any information which might be useful to the enemy. Many Red Cross forms can be seen to have been examined for secret writing as they have been marked with a chemical wash.

Sometimes it is difficult to imagine why a sentence was thought to be objectionable. Kathleen Nowlan received a message from a friend in England in May 1942 and, as was usual, typed a reply clearly on the back. It read 'March message received. Both well and busy. Great hopes for future. Love. Chum.' This must have seemed to her harmless enough but the German censor went to the trouble of neatly cutting a hole in the form to remove the words 'Great hopes for future.'

However there is evidence that censorship was patchy and many messages were probably never examined at all by a censor.

Most messages were straightforward with no hidden meanings but the fact that some refugees were talking about their coded news caused everyone to examine the Red Cross forms with great care. 'Messages are eagerly scanned, their words carefully examined and weighed, and every comparison is made with available scraps of news,' wrote A.D. Creighton in the Stockport Review for August 1942.

This attitude led some people to puzzle for days over what was perhaps a harmless omission or mistake. R.N. Ingram of Guernsey appealed for help when he received a message in April 1942 from his friend Lloyd Robilliard, who worked in the National Provincial Bank, which included the sentence, 'Have you no socks.' He was sure that this concealed a deeper statement but nobody could suggest that it meant anything other than that the sender wished be could obtain new socks.

In another message the words 'learning French gardening' puzzled the recipient until it was realised that the writer probably intended to put a comma after the word French.

In September 1943 Roy Carre was puzzled by a message from his brother Lloyd in Guernsey that, 'Dad, Gerald, Tom myself looking like schoolmasters.' He appealed for help and the only suggestion was that it meant they looked shabby and was an allusion to the fact that schoolmasters were not usually affluent.

'Getting allowance on S.L.I. address.' This was even more puzzling for Mrs Harris when this sentence was included in a message from her sister in Guernsey in December 1942.

Several messages mentioned that the sender was 'gathering Carrageen' or 'eating seaweed.' and at first these both puzzled and worried some of the refugees but it was soon pointed out at CI meetings that 'Carrageen', a marine plant, was well known in Ireland where it was used extensively in coastal regions for making blancmange or jelly.

After the war an enduring memory for many people on both sides of the Channel was the deeply emotional effect the Red Cross messages had for some. In her autobiography about her Jersey youth *A Garland of Daisies*, Mrs Margaret Vaudin wrote,

> It was ten months before we received a message from England through the Red Cross. It consisted of twenty-five words and was six months old...The first came from my sister who had a really very tough war, not knowing how we were faring. Poor Postman Counter was so thrilled to bring us a message, and was quite shattered when I burst into tears before I even opened it. It was wonderful to get a message but they were so brief and frustrating. We were longing to hear some real news of all our relatives and friends in England. My father used to say, "I don't understand you. You curse when you receive a message and you curse when you don't." It was not strictly true but very nearly so.

Nan Le Ruez's diary provides several other examples. She too was in Jersey, a girl in her 20s deeply in love with her fiancé, Alfred, who lived in England. 'What a joy it is to receive these messages, short and late as they are,' she wrote on 4 March 1942.

But when in the following year Alfred said in one of his messages, "I am weary of long and needless separation," she interpreted this as 'so cold, no love' and the words made her so miserable that she couldn't sleep, was off her food and was fearful of going to chapel in case she should break down in public. Then, later in the month, she received another message 'I thank God that I've had a message from Alfred. The fact that he sent one gives me relief. I was…in the garden when Mother told me there was a message for me. I found myself trembling…I knelt down to pray for strength before opening it.' (30 October, 1943).

The total number of messages which went to and from the Channel Islands is not known precisely. According to Ralph Mollet who was Secretary to the Jersey Bailiff during the occupation, Jersey alone received and answered 235,744 and 92,041 messages originated there on forms supplied by the German Red Cross.

The Red Cross employed hundreds of people to organise the despatch and delivery of these small printed enquiry forms on which people wrote their brief messages. At the time it must have seemed to some of the workers that they were making a negligible contribution to the war effort. But as a humanitarian effort it contributed a great deal to the morale and well-being of thousands of people.

GUERNSEY CALLS TO SICILY

O, island of flowers, of vines and of olives,
Old castles and churches that Normans of old
Left for a memory of the time they possessed you.
Each one bears a tale that has never been told.
Our island possess old castles and churches,
And we also like you are captives of war.
If only someone would ease us of burdens,
As our brave soldiers are bringing you law.
The Normans once ruled you, but we, too, are Normans:
In bygone days we were under their law.
O, island of Sicily, this is our greeting:
The Normans are coming to free you once more.

by Jean Taylor, aged 12, at the time of the
Sicilian campaign (November 1943)

Chapter 10

Daily Life

For today, to remind you of the infinite love watching over our loved ones and ourselves, to acknowledge with thanksgiving that we have found kindly friends as well as hardship in our time of exile . For the coming days the remembrance that even this time of distress has brought its own enriching experience, not yet to be measured or understood. THIS BOOK ...is sent to bring to you its own word of strength.

Inscription printed in Bibles which were signed and given to
CI refugees by the Methodist ministers, R. D. Moore and
George Whitley when they visited local CI societies.

Some people cope well with change. For others their new surroundings, and a different routine coupled with the need to adapt and face unfamiliar problems, was a traumatic experience which left unpleasant memories or worse for the rest of their lives.

The separation from their parents and the long journey with strangers was hard on children below the age of about 10 and especially distressing for infants around six years of age.

It was a disagreeable experience for many, both children and adults, to be billeted with complete strangers. Although the practice of lining children up so that they could be examined and picked as if they were goods on a market stall before billeting was less common than it had been in the big evacuation of September 1939, there were still some who experienced a selection procedure of some kind. It is noticeable that in many biographical accounts written years later by adults who evacuated they frequently claim to have been the last, or very nearly the last, to have been chosen. If their memories were correct and they really were the last the experience had clearly left a long-lasting sour taste. But perhaps their recollection was not accurate and they simply felt that they were one of the last and therefore least attractive because of the slowness of the proceedings and the overlying anxiety.

Betty Moore left Guernsey at the age of ten with St. Andrews School and lived communally in a church hall in Eccles for three weeks before her school class was taken to Irby, a small town near Birkenhead. Here she was billeted with a young couple. The second day in the small house was her birthday and she was given a red ball.

By now I realised my parents would not be coming, and often I cried myself to sleep. A few months later my brother (aged 20) who was stationed in Wales, came to see me. He was in Army uniform and had grown a moustache but I could not recognise him.

Then Betty's foster parents announced that they were expecting their first baby and told the billeting officer she would have to go. Betty was taken to her second billet, this time in Heswall so that she had a two-mile walk to school, which by this time was divided between Irby and Barnston.

At night they could hear bombs falling on Liverpool and Birkenhead only five miles away and on one occasion a bomb hit houses in Barnston so her foster parents decided to leave the district and Betty was billeted yet again, this time with a middle-aged woman and her elderly mother in Heswall. "I was treated more as a servant and made to do a lot of housework," says Betty.

It was policy for an official to visit homes where children were billeted and after a time Betty asked her billeting officer whether she could be moved elsewhere. Now her luck changed and she found herself on a farm at Barnston where there were two young sons in the family and the farmer's wife "was the lovely lady who cooked the school dinners."

Betty's life was happier now. She remained on the farm for the war years and eventually left school and worked in an office, with her foster mother paying for her to attend classes in shorthand and typing.

Betty's experience emphasises the strong element of chance that attached itself to the lives of evacuated children. She was lucky to become part of a happy household and this was the experience of a large number of the evacuees. Others were made to join families with which for various reasons they never felt comfortable.

The employment of young children on farms was not uncommon during the war and was permitted by law. The Children and Young Persons Act laid down prescribed hours when children could work but of course this was impossible to enforce.

John and Alf Lainé of Guernsey were 10-year old twins when they left the island with Hautes Capelles school. They were more fortunate than others because their mother was with the school party as one of the helpers but nevertheless when they were arrived in Wigan they found themselves billeted separately from their mother. The school was then divided between three Cheshire villages: Ridley Green, Bunbury and Spurstow. The twins were now billeted on a farm in Ridley and enjoyed life on the farm but at harvest time were made to work and were kept away from school until the schools inspector visited the farm. When their mother who was living in Bunbury, heard about this she arranged for them to be billeted in the same village with the family of a lorry driver. After a year the twins were separated. Alf was sent to Elizabeth College in Derby and John to the Intermediate School at Oldham where he was placed in yet another billet, the home of William Hughes a draughtsman in a factory who was also a Methodist preacher.

It was a comfortable home but on the night of 12 October 1941 a bomb struck the house. He and two members of the family were buried in the debris and survived but the others were killed.

The use of children for farm labour is remembered too by Olive Quin, a married woman of 25 who evacuated with her baby Carol and was living in Burnley when she had a Red Cross message from her brother in Guernsey asking her if she knew where her nephew, Tommy, aged five, was now living. She had no idea where Tommy's school had gone so she wrote to the Channel Islands Refugees Committee in London and had a reply giving her the address of a farm near Nantwich where Tommy was billeted. Months later Olive was able to raise enough money to pay for the fare to Nantwich.

She was dismayed to find that Tommy was being made to work long hours:

>...he had to be up at 5.30 a.m., feed the chickens, get the cows in for milking and then go in for his breakfast, after which he had to do the washing up before he went off to school.

He was clearly not only unhappy but unwell too so she insisted on taking him back to Burnley.

Several other evacuees who were schoolchildren at the time tell stories of being made to work on farms or to do excessive domestic work in their billets.

Making a home

In contrast to unpleasant experiences of bombs, shortages and exploitation are the memories of some adult evacuees who were able to find rented accommodation and satisfactory jobs.

Most of the younger adults seem to have found employment fairly easily and it was not too difficult to find some sort of rented accommodation. But, as Leslie Picot points out in his autobiography *Living through the London Blitz* ,

>to establish a home from scratch was exceedingly difficult as new furnishings were few and far between. A points system was in operation to help bombed-out people and newly weds. We attended many auction sales and studied newspaper for sale columns.

But outside London home-making was easier. A.R. Keeling, who was founder and secretary of the Penzance CI Society, remembers groups of Guernsey people coming from the north to Penzance and jointly renting some of the large houses that were available there during the war.

Margaret Hocquard (now Mrs Newman) who was seven in 1940 remembers travelling on 20 June 1940 on one of the last flights out of Jersey, sitting on her parents' knees. Her father, Ted Hocquard, and his brother, had an electrical business in Jersey, with a shop in Beresford Street.

Her grandmother lived in Oxford so the family lodged there until Mr Hocquard, within two weeks, was able to rent a house in Oxford. Both he and his brother found employment in the local factory of Pressed Steel Co which was then making aircraft bodies.

Margaret went to school in Oxford throughout the war and remembers no particular problems. She recalls that

> ...it was considered slightly more prestigious to be a 'refugee' rather than an 'evacuee'. There were a lot of Jewish refugees from Europe so at school there were other children with strange names and accents. As a Jersey child who could speak English without an accent, German or cockney, I had an advantage.

W. A. Bisson was nine when he left Jersey with his mother, Margaret and his aunt, Amy Blampied. His mother was a waitress in a restaurant in Dumaresq Street and his aunt a housemaid. They arrived in Rochdale with other evacuees and were soon able to rent an empty house (31, Red Lane). As with so many other evacuees they were given enough furniture and household items by neighbours to make a home. His mother obtained a job as a shop assistant for a local grocer, James Duckworth, and his aunt got work in the local laundry.

Mr Bisson writes:

> We soon settled down to an ordinary life, if there can be one in wartime, and we were accepted after a while by the locals. I sang in the choir at All Saints Church, Hamer, and won a scholarship to Rochdale High School for Boys. At first, because of our Jersey accent, we were thought of as being rather posh, and it was a while before we understood some of the Lancashire dialect. I still have great affection for Rochdale and Lancashire in general. The people were rough and ready but were very kind to us in our moment of need.

Ann Gibaut (now Mrs Bissell-Thomas) was a 12 year old farmer's daughter in Jersey at the time of the evacuation. Her father took her and her mother to the airport and managed to get two seats on one of the last flights but Mr Gibaut remained in Jersey and was there during the Occupation.

They arrived in Bristol and stayed a night at a hotel. Mrs Gibaut had very little money. Although Bristol was bombed that night Ann remembers having no fear, only a sense that it was a big adventure. The next day they went to relatives at Barnstable, then to Isleworth in London, where there was more heavy bombing in September 1940.

On 12 October 1940 they went to St Mawes, a fishing village in Cornwall, about 5 miles south of Truro where they were able to stay with two cousins. A bank manager in Falmouth agreed to make a monthly allowance of about £10 to Mrs Gibaut, just enough to live on, on condition it was paid back after the war. Another relative, Aunt Jessie Luce, who wanted to help refugees, had offered to pay the school fees of a Guernsey child and now she agreed to pay Ann's too. This enabled Ann to attend a girls' school in Truro for the remainder of the war.

It was a happy, Jersey household, she says, often with much Jersey-French being spoken, and apart from the deep worries of not knowing what was going on in Jersey and how her father was getting on, she was comfortably looked after.

Social Life

Reference has already been made to the large number of Societies for Channel Islanders which formed in many parts of the country.

Daily life for many refugees was a struggle to make ends meet in drab and inadequate accommodation. But a meeting of their local CI society was often the one bright spot in the week.

Hundreds of Channel Islanders dedicated themselves to running a local group, arranging meetings, raising money for various causes or for parties and socials at festive seasons and planning outings for CI children throughout the year.

We have a glimpse of what the meetings meant in a speech by the chairman of the Croydon CI Society, Mr R. Hamilton Farrell, when he attended the first meeting of the Woolwich Society on 28 July 1943:

> I have found that the Croydon members are interested in social gatherings and listening to speakers talking about the Islands, but above all they love to talk about the islands themselves. Although Societies like ours are social affairs in public they give a great deal of help and comfort to Channel Islanders, whether members of the Society or not.

Some refugees took pleasure in travelling about the country especially to attend a meeting of a Society other than their own. On Sunday 23 August 1942 about 200 members of the Stockport CI Society were met at Bolton Station by members of the Bolton CI Society and then proceeded to walk in a long crocodile to a local hall.

Entertainment groups with a recognisably CI name also travelled about the country. The 'Corbiere Coons' based in Wakefield entertained with minstrel songs and dances. The Manchester Society had a troupe called 'Island Follies' which gave regular concerts. In Halifax the Guernsey Society encouraged their members to entertain by arranging afternoons known as 'Sing, Say or Pay'

Children's parties, sometimes with several hundred children, usually in December or January were highly successful events for many societies. Many of these parties, as well as summer outings to seaside places such as Blackpool and Southport were supported financially by the Channel Islands Refugees Committee. The local Mayor or other prominent citizen often put in an appearance on these occasions. In Plymouth on 16 December 1943, Lady Astor distributed presents to 70 Channel Island children at their Christmas party and each child received an apple and a sixpence. Local charities sometimes provided toys for the parties. When 200 CI children attended the 1943 Christmas party in Bath they were given toys which had been made by local firemen during their 'stand by' time in the local fire station.

It seems clear from the hundreds of enthusiastic reports of these Channel Island meetings and events during the war that the companionship, the social activity, the involvement with welfare projects, the sense of kinship and identifying with an extended family, resulted in many refugees having the time of their lives.

Pre-war books about the Channel Islands, and all kinds of pictures of Channel Island views, were much sought after by the refugees. They were frequently displayed, exchanged or sold at CI meetings. Ted Hamel recalls in his memoirs that he once found an old CI holiday guide on a second-hand market stall in Bradford. 'As the years passed,' he writes, 'the photographs in that book were worth more to us than all the pictures in the National Gallery. It was borrowed time and again, and reluctantly returned. No book was ever more thumbed in the space of five years.'

Enforced separation from their homeland caused people to think about it more intensively, with (perhaps exaggerated) affection, and with a greater longing. Although not a refugee, R.R. Marett noticed this when in 1942 he wrote in his autobiography, 'being cut off from Jersey has urged me to translate my longing for the scenes of my youth into explicit recollection of their manifold delights...'

Radio programmes mentioning the CIs were a source of much pleasure to the refugees. On Christmas Day, 1941 there was a nostalgic 20-minute broadcast at 11.40 a.m. in the Forces programme of the BBC, simply titled The Channel Islands. *The Radio Times* described it as 'Programme with music for those who have known and loved the islands.'

Among those taking part were Edward O'Henry, Edward Hocquard, Betty Wood-Hall, Muriel Luckie and Daryl Querée. In Jersey, both Leslie Sinel and Nan Le Ruez noted the broadcast in their diaries. Sinel expressed everybody's disappointment "that no actual message was sent." He could not have known that some of the refugees had asked for personal messages to be included but after consulting the Home office the BBC decided it was inadvisable to direct the broadcast to people in occupied territory. A similar programme was broadcast in the Home Service on Christmas Day, 1942.

Badges

Channel Islanders not only liked to meet each other but wanted to be identified as refugees as they went about their daily routine. In June 1942 Mrs F. Lucy of Hollingbourne wrote to the CI Review: 'Would it be feasible for Channel Islanders to have a badge–just the letters CI?' She quoted an occasion when she had travelled 30 miles by bus and only discovered at the end of the journey that another passenger was a fellow islander. 'If only we had known before!'

This brought a response from Victor Coysh suggesting that if a Guernsey 'farthing' (or a Jersey coin) were 'properly polished and mounted on a pin' it would make an ideal badge. However in Barnsley the CI Society had already placed an order with a local manufacturer for several hundred small metal badges. As soon as this was made known

Channel Islanders were keen to meet each other and thousands of badges like this were sold during the War.

they received requests from numerous societies. When 70 members the Guildford CI Society met on 14 March 1943 every member placed an order for a badge. By May 1 it was reported that 'demand for the CI badges is unprecedented' and more were being ordered from the manufacturer. Orders continued to be made by Society secretaries throughout 1943 and 1944. By the end of 1944 the supply had evidently run out for the Secretary of the Oxford CI Society placed an advertisement in the *CI Review*: 'Has anyone CI badges for sale?'

The total number of CI badges made during the war is not known but it must have run into thousands. The accounts of the Channel Islands Refugees Committee for the year ended 30 June 1944 include an item 'Cost of badges...£335.' Some Societies announced that the price of a badge was 11d so the CIRC must have handled about 8,000 during only one year.

Today specimens of these badges are scarce. In the summer of 1994 the author asked several dealers in Channel Island ephemera if they could supply one and all reported that such badges are rarely seen and are much sought after by collectors.

Northern towns and cities seemed drab to the refugees. Even the wartime trams were painted grey.

The image published during the war of happy exiled children in northern schools was only partly true. Since the war stories of exploitation on farms and unhappy times in billets have been told. The following is part of an editorial in the *Channel Islands Monthly Review* published on 1 September 1943 in Stockport:

With the Children

GUERNSEY mothers will be proud of their children when the time comes for their welcome home, and none should regret that hasty passive consent to entrust them to the care of their school teachers when, over three years ago, they embarked for England's hospitable shores. The pangs of sudden parting and the anxieties caused by long separation will be alleviated by the realisation that the youngsters have grown up in a manner which the parents would have wished, and in many cases above their normal expectations.

A great and noble work has been going on these three years and more, away from all limelight, and without thought of reward apart perhaps from satisfaction at performing a duty conscientiously and well. That duty has entailed multiple responsibility for the teachers who, having promised to look after their young charges, have never wavered in the dual role of tutor and guardian.

To single out any individual or school may seem invidious, but what appears below can be taken as typical of conditions in most parts of the country where Guernsey children are schooled. It was with the paramount idea of making personal contact with children whose parents remained at home that a visit to the district with the largest contingent was undertaken just before the holidays. It happened to be the Vale School, but its scholars were distributed over nine villages in Council and Church schools along with Cheshire children. However, we were fortunate to descend upon the Headmaster, Mr. R. E. Carré, just as he was about to set out on one of his periodic tours, with the back of his car stacked with clothing for distribution, and gladly accepted his invitation to accompany him.

In an informal surprise visit, amid beautiful rural settings, the children were seen at various schools at their studies, at play, or at work on some of the best regulated farms in Cheshire. There were not quite so many as we had expected to see, due to the fact that some had been claimed by relatives residing in other counties, but those who remained bore unmistakable testimony that they were in very good hands. Almost without exception they were the embodiment of robust health, content, and imbued with a sound spirit of thrift.

At the first school the youngsters were treasuring their recently purchased savings stamps, at another they told of bank balances of from £11 to over £20. In addition one young gentleman owned three pigs, others rabbits or poultry, while more had their own patch of ground to till after school hours. Their savings are derived mostly from part-time light work on neighbouring farms, occupations which they obviously enjoy, with the whole-hearted encouragement of the foster-parents with whom they are billeted, and always with the approval of their moral guardians the teachers. We saw several of these foster-parents, who are perhaps more attached to their temporary orphans than are the children themselves, whose love must perforce be divided between Mum and Dad at home and 'Uncle' and 'Auntie' of Cheshire.

"How many of you will not shed a tear when the day comes to go back home?" was a question put to a large party of Sarnian scholars.

"Oh!" was the spontaneous chorus, and not a hand went up. All want to go back, of course, but just a few intend to return afterwards to settle in the land that gave them so many happy days when the world was in tumult.

There was no evidence of home-sickness among the many with whom we had heart to heart talks. They were too interested in their tasks, with no time to brood over what might have been. Still they cherished the endearing and inspiring [Red Cross] messages received occasionally from the Vale and St. Sampson's. On recalling that a brother or sister over there had found a good job one could almost read the workings of those young minds—they seemed determined to do likewise eventually, or perhaps better. With the right training, combined with a developed strength of character and an outlook already far removed from insularity, they appeared to be tolerably well equipped to aspire to success. Some discussed their prospects of winning scholarships, while a few were on the point of leaving school. Situations were not hard to find, but anything was not good enough for young people soon destined to take a hand in assisting their island to regain prosperity. Blind-alley ventures were not to be thought of. So judicious advice was imparted with a view to placing the youths and young girls in posts of prospect, with due regard to ability and natural bent.

RETURN

The Day will come for which I pray,
When I shall leave this friendly shore,
And tread the road where, in dismay,
I came in exile years before.
But this time with a lighter heart,
Back to my Island home once more
From which I've been so long apart;
To see the loved ones I adore.
To grasp the hands I yearn to hold,
And eye meet eye in anxious gaze,
And in a fond embrace enfold
Forgetting all those weary days.
And though the seas be angry then,
With such a peace within my soul
I'll fear not troubled waters when
I look towards that distant goal.
At length with vision misty-wet
Behold in joyous ecstasy
The Isles in blessed silhouette
Stand bravely out against the sea!

by A. R. Keeling, 1944
(This poem was specially written to be printed on the back
of the membership cards of the Penzance and District
Channel Islands Society)

Chapter 11

Looking into the future

Thousands of islanders who were evacuated to Britain will have learned other ways. There will no doubt be those who wish to rehabilitate the old system as completely as possible; others will plead for innovations in various directions.

Nos Iles, March 1944.

Towards the end of 1942 a new spirit of optimism was growing in Britain. When the El Alamein victory in North Africa was announced on 10 November Winston Churchill said in the Commons, "It is not the end, it is not even the beginning of the end. But it is perhaps the end of the beginning."

The nation felt that the tide of the war was turning and the refugees began to think that an imminent return to the islands was a possibility. Lord Justice du Parcq, writing in the *CI Monthly Review* on 1 January 1943, said, "Whether we may now discern, however dimly, the beginning of the end I will not say, but at any rate we are all confident, and confident with good reason, that the end will be not only peace but victory and for each of you not only a homecoming but a return to an Island freed and cleansed, and ready to welcome you as free men and women. Let it be your hope and your prayer that 1943 will see the great day of reunion."

In the summer of 1940 the author J.B. Priestley gave short weekly radio talks (called the Sunday Postscript) which became increasingly political in tone. He talked about 'a better England' in the future and how people 'can plan and create a noble future for all our species.' Priestley's talks were immensely popular and it seems likely that they sowed the seeds of new attitudes to social change.

December 1942 saw the publication of the Beveridge report, proposals for social security which are recognised today as the beginning of the 'welfare state'. A mood of political radicalism was by now widespread in Britain and was strongly influencing the thinking of Channel Islanders as they looked forward to their return. The pages of the *CI Monthly Review* contain many letters from islanders who wanted to see social changes. Early in 1943 the social welfare being talked about included free medical and hospital treatment for everyone, a retirement pension for all, and family allowances. In March 1943 Norman Grut wrote to the *Review*:

Post-war planning will and must occupy the minds of all Channel Islanders...The Beveridge plan is approved by 90 per cent of the people here, and should be introduced into the islands, although of course the people there and the States of both Jersey and Guernsey have not yet had an opportunity of seeing it. Let us hope that the day is not far distant.

Several letters supported this view but there were also words of caution, mainly from people who said that the economy of the islands would not be able to support welfare services of the sort envisaged in the Beveridge report. When Lord Justice du Parcq spoke to Channel Islanders at a public meeting in Bath on 22 May 1943 he warned of the danger of taking back to the islands a ready-made plan for the post-war period. "Nothing," he said, "would be more calculated to cause bad feeling between those who left and those who remained."

In fact a 'plan', or rather a collection of essays on the future of the Channel Islands would soon be in print. It was called *Nos Iles*.

The suggestion which led to this was first put forward by Professor H.J. Fleure (1877-1969), a Guernseyman who was Professor of Geography at the University of Manchester. He wrote on 20 May 1941 to the Secretary of the Jersey Society in London, Derek du Pré:

> I very much hope that the Societies relating to the islanders in England can work together. I have in mind that a number of us should co-operate to issue a book that would give rather serious information in fairly simple form to enlighten public opinion on the Channel Islands problem...Of people who could be concerned in some way with the issue of such a book I might mention Lord Justice du Parcq, Mr Le Quesne, yourself, Dr Marett, Dr Mourant, Mr Warren, Mr J.P. Collas and myself. The last three would be concerned more especially with Guernsey and the smaller islands and the others more particularly with Jersey.

Derek du Pré joined the Army not long after this letter was written and his place as secretary to the Jersey Society in London was taken by Philip de Veulle. As the national optimism of 1943 began to grow, de Veulle arranged for what he called a 'Re-Union Conference' to be held at Jesus College, Oxford during the week-end of 10/11 July 1943. Several delegates presented discussion papers and at the end of the conference six study groups were set up to prepare papers for publication by the end of September. Philip de Veulle took on the task of co-ordinating the project and in March 1944 published the papers in *Nos Iles, A Symposium on the Channel Islands*, a book of 70,000 words.

It was an immediate success and after it had been mentioned in the Stockport CI Review the first printing of 1,000 copies sold within a few weeks at 3/6d each. A reprint was advertised in September 1944.

A copy was sent to Buckingham Palace. The King's private secretary acknowledged it on 5 May 1944 when he wrote to Major-General Sir Donald Banks as chairman of the Study Group,

> I have laid before the King the copy of Nos Iles which you are good enough to send for His Majesty's acceptance.
>
> The King is very glad to have this little book, which gives such a comprehensive account of the Channel Islands in which, as you know, he is always deeply interested. His Majesty trusts, no less than you do, that the day may not be far distant when the Channel Islands are once more clear of the enemy. Yours sincerely, A. Lascelles.

The book was reprinted several times and after the Liberation copies were sent to all members of the States of Jersey and Guernsey, creating considerable interest and eventually being referred to as the 'Liberation Army's Bible.'

We get some idea of what was in the minds of the refugees from a report on a Channel Island conference which took place in Huddersfield on 14 April 1944. 400 delegates attended, mostly from CI Societies in the north of England. The first subject discussed was the future of education in the islands after the war. Several Societies pressed for information about government plans for the return of the refugees, especially whether transport would be available for their newly acquired furniture and other possessions. There was much criticism of the British government for, as one delegate put it, 'withholding information' about plans for the CIs. There was discussion about welfare services in the islands after the war. Many wanted to know whether the Beveridge report would be adopted by the States. 'Holidays with pay will be the big thing after the war,' said one delegate.

Delegates at CI Conference in Oxford on 10 July 1943

Brigadier Sir Donald Banks (Guernsey)
Air Commodore H. Le M. Brock (Guernsey)
Major J.S. Crill (Jersey)
Philip de Veulle (Jersey)
Col. F.G. French (Alderney)
R.F.B. Gaudin (Jersey)
A.B. Grayson (Jersey)
Barry Jones (Guernsey)
Dr John Le Patourel (Guernsey)
Dr Arthur Mourant (Jersey)
Albert Messervy (Jersey)
Sir Herbert du Parcq PC (Jersey)
C.T. Le Quesne KC, (Jersey)
R.H.K. Marett (Jersey)

'A Universal Thrill'

Soon after D-Day on the 6 June 1944, the *CI Review* expressed the feeling of the refugees boldly in a front page editorial:

> News of the invasion of Normandy, after weeks of tension and patient waiting, came as a universal thrill, tempered by some degree of anxiety...To us all it heralds the great day of liberation...

Few who read those words in the summer of 1944 imagined that at least another year would pass before most refugees could return to their island homes.

The Channel Islands Refugees Committee began to get an overwhelming number of enquiries about the return to the islands. Some even asked where they could buy tickets for the first sailing, and whether they could send luggage in advance.

In reply to all these questions the CIRC sent a printed circular (No. 54) pointing out that 'no one knows under what conditions reoccupation will take place, and what the state of the islands will be.'

It was pointed out that the demands on shipping would be tremendous and there was no likelihood that at an early date shipping would be available to start a passenger service. 'It must also be remembered,' the circular went on, 'that much will have to be done in the islands before they are really habitable by their present inhabitants, and still more before they can receive back those refugees now in the United Kingdom.'

Such was the growing concern that refugees began to write to MPs and on 6 July the Home Secretary, Herbert Morrison, made a statement in the House of Commons confirming that plans had been prepared for dealing with the situation in the Channel Islands when their liberation was achieved, but until full information as to the conditions in the islands was available it was not possible to forecast the steps to be taken for the return of islanders.

A week after D-Day the first of many thousands of flying bombs (or doodle-bugs) began to drop on England, particularly in the south-east. Croydon, where there were many CI refugees, received 141, more than any other part of the London area. In Maidstone on Saturday 1 July the sound of gunfire interrupted the meeting of the Channel Islands Society of Kent. A doodle-bug fell near the hall, bringing the meeting to a close, but it resumed later in the afternoon.

As the year progressed with no sign of liberation the refugees became more and more anxious about the conditions in the islands.

The November editorial in the *CI Review* expressed the thoughts of Islanders:

> Far behind the line of battle the Channel Islands remain under German subjection, and the question asked on all sides is: How much longer? If their liberation does not come soon the plight of those loyal and brave islanders will cause the greatest concern. We

are led to believe that their food stocks can tide them over until the end of November, and that medical supplies are an urgent necessity.

During the autumn a number of young men had managed to escape from Jersey to France in small boats. The London newspapers began to publish lurid stories of hardship and near starvation in the islands. MPs again raised the subject in the Commons and Lord Portsea asked more questions in the Lords about the Norman Islands, as he always called them.

Late in November rumours began to circulate that the Red Cross was ready to send food supplies to the islands. A Reuter message from Lisbon on 28 November said that over a million food parcels were waiting to be shipped and the *Daily Telegraph* reported that the British Red Cross had confirmed that parcels would be sent from Lisbon.

The arrival of the Red Cross ship *Vega* on 27 December with food parcels for all the civilian populations of the two Bailiwicks is still celebrated in the islands even today, 50 years after the event. The news was released in Britain on New Year's Day 1945. To the CI refugees in the UK it was a great emotional relief to know that at last something had been done to help their besieged relatives and friends. It was the most talked about topic at excited meetings of CI Societies all over the country. Someone in the London area managed to get hold of a specimen Canadian Red Cross Food parcel with contents and this was displayed at several meetings, including the Kingston and Croydon societies during February and March.

But of course this did not bring any closer the day when they could sail home. Many were so convinced that it would not be long that they began to move to the south coast in the hope that they would be among the first to get to the liberated islands. This trend prompted the secretary of the Weymouth CI Society, Percy H. de Louche, to write in January to the *CI Review* appealing for Channel Islanders not to travel to the south coast. He was receiving applications for houses, flats or other apartments and he wished 'to emphasise the great shortage of accommodation in these areas. The fact of being resident in these ports is not likely to influence in any way the prospects of obtaining priority in returning to the islands.' The CIRC issue yet another circular (No. 57) warning Channel Islanders that 'they should not leave their employment, nor give up their homes, nor proceed to a port of embarkation without first referring to the British Government.'

Moving Service at the Abbey

On Sunday 30 April, 1944, a warm and sunny day, a special service for Channel Islanders was held in Westminster Abbey. 2,000 people managed to obtain seats and large numbers stood in the Nave. In the congregation was the Minister of Health, Henry U. Willink, MP, and leading members of the CIRC and WVS. The Dean, the Right Rev Dr. Paul de Labilliere (1879-1946), who had lived in Jersey as a child, spoke movingly, his text being from Luke 21,28, 'look up, and lift up your heads, for your redemption draweth near.'

Let me say at once that it is with feeling of profound sympathy and respect that we welcome to our Abbey this great congregation, composed in the main of our fellow subjects from the Channel Islands who have been driven from their homes by the cruel and wanton invasion of our common enemy. You are a congregation of exiles...all exiles speak a universal language, the language of the homesickness of the soul. You meet it again and again in history, in literature and in life...

Ten thousand of your kith and kin are serving today in the armed forces of the Crown, men without homes, whose families are in many cases under the Nazi heel...

I want to end, if I may, on a note of thankfulness and hope. Not for a moment do we forget all the sufferings and humiliation you have been called upon to endure. But in spite of your protracted ordeal your spirit has remained, as all who knew you anticipated that it would, buoyant, challenging and undismayed. Hundreds of your fellow islanders have suffered deportation...while 30,000 of you have found shelter on our shores as welcomed and honoured guests. I do not hesitate to say that by your spirit of deathless courage and indomitable hope you have made a real contribution to our national morale. The C.I. Refugees Committee has done wonders in the way of mitigating distress, and planning and preparing for your return.

Chapter 12

Going Home

… there was one person he really loved: that was his daughter. He had let her be evacuated so as she would be safe, as he thought. He was only living for the happiness of having her home again. She was safe all right; but the people she was put to live with in England didn't have any children of their own and, when the time came for her to come home, they wanted to keep her. In the meantime she had forgotten Guernsey and her father and got into English ways and wanted to stay with 'Mum and Dad.' They was well-to-do people and could give her everything of the best.

from *The Book of Ebenezer le Page* by G.B. Edwards

Ted Hamel watched the excited Bradford crowds celebrating the end of the war in Europe on 8 May, 1945. He waited half the night in the hope of hearing something on the radio about the Channel Islands. The German surrender of the islands was not signed until 9 May and then not announced until the 1 p.m. news on BBC radio. Hamel described the excitement of his family

The news bulletin at 6 p.m. on that day was more important than a meal. Even the youngsters sensed the importance of silence. We learned that the surrender of the enemy forces had been received on a destroyer in the roads outside St Peter Port. The recording of that event, which followed the news, was to us the greatest broadcast ever! It was moving in the extreme and technically perfect. The lapping of the water could be clearly heard as the launch carrying the German commander drew alongside. The BBC did a grand job. I doubt if the producer of that recording realised that he had received enough blessings in those few minutes to put him on the short list for a seat in heaven. We sat there…not knowing whether to laugh or cry. Then came the questions. [The recording was by the BBC War Correspondent Douglas Willis].

In the days which followed it was an enormous disappointment, although not unexpected, for many refugees to find that they were not permitted to return to the islands immediately. Others, having made new lives for themselves, sometimes in better paid jobs and better accommodation than they had had before the war, did not want to return, at least for the time being. In Bury, where 50 new houses on the Chesham estate had been occupied by CI refugees in 1940, there were still eight CI families occupying seven of the houses by March 1947. When the billeting authority was disbanded at that time all except one of these families decided that they preferred to remain as Bury citizens.

The CIRC was getting so many enquiries that the Director, M. E. Weatherall went to Manchester on 3 June to attend a meeting of nearly 6,000 refugees arranged by the Manchester & District CI Society at Belle Vue. He said that he did not know when the refugees could return to their islands and he went on to give a rather exaggerated view of the conditions. Houses and hotels which had been occupied by troops were 'in an appalling state of filth, distribution of clothing had only just begun, there had been much damage to property and many houses needed repairing before they could be reoccupied. Many fields were both covered in barbed wire and mined.' He said it was 'excessively improbable that there would be anything like a general return in the near future,'

When he got back to London Weatherall immediately issued an official CIRC circular in which he wrote

> The immediate return to the Islands of a large number of persons would create very serious problems of accommodation and unemployment, and at the outset provision can be made for the return of only a few hundred persons per week. Later the rate will increase as employment and accommodation become available. The Island authorities will be responsible for allotting priorities, and persons who will be selected for early return will be Channel islanders for whom there is immediate employment in the Islands and those who have homes to go to and whose re-absorption will not create local problems. There will be no question of holiday-makers visiting the islands this year. Returning residents will be allowed to take with them a reasonable amount of luggage but household goods will have to be sent by cargo steamer...

The return of the population of Alderney is being considered separately and these arrangements do not apply to Alderney.

Residents who wanted to return to the islands had to apply by post (not in person) to the passport office in London. If a permit was granted it was possible to obtain a free passage by making an application to the billeting officer of your district.

If you were successful in getting an exit permit there was still the problem of getting tickets for crossing the channel. The Southern Railway mailboat service from Southampton did not start until 25 June, and then it made the crossing only three times a week. An air service by Jersey Airways also began in June, flying twice a day from Jersey to Croydon via Guernsey but the capacity of the aircraft was less than twenty for each flight.

For Ted Hamel and his family the summer of 1945 was one of great frustration. As a telephone engineer his services were badly wanted in Guernsey so employment presented no problem. He owned a house in Guernsey. But still he couldn't get a permit from the passport office. He even travelled to London to visit the office in person but still no permit was forthcoming.

It came in October. When the family arrived at Bradford railway station for the start of the journey homeward it was to find that

> There were Guernseyman with Yorkshire wives. Yorkshiremen with Guernsey wives. There were Yorkshire born children of Guernsey parentage setting off for the new home across the sea...There were push carts and toys, babies and bottles, and as we entered the train not a few moist eyes at the parting with the many staunch friends we had all made in those memorable years.

They crossed the channel on the pre-war mailboat the *Isle of Jersey*, which had been a hospital ship throughout the war and had only been handed back to Southern Railway on 10 October. As she moved slowly into the harbour of St Peter Port nothing seemed to have changed, said Ted Hamel, except for a concrete bunker at the pierhead, 'but the skyline had the same bumps in the same places: Victoria Tower, St James', Elizabeth College, Castle Carey...' And the faces of the people who had come to meet them were thin and bronzed compared with those on board the ship.

Later, in the town, he was struck by the cleanliness of everything compared with what he had become used to in Bradford. 'Even faded paint was clean, as if it had been freshly scrubbed for our return.'

He knew from the coded Red Cross messages which he had received that his house had been taken over by Germans. Now he found it so vandalised and filthy that many weeks of work would be necessary to make it habitable. In 1940 it had been completely furnished; now it contained only two items of furniture: a bedside lamp and kitchen linoleum which was so dirty that it could not be seen. But the excitement of the return after more than five years meant that 'Nothing of this mattered one hoot – we were home!'

Victor Coysh returned to Guernsey on 25 October 1945 and recorded in his diary, 'My joy at seeing it was unbounded. I missed the Doyle and Delancey monuments but little else seemed altered.'

Olive Quin, too, remembers the excitement of her homecoming in the summer of 1945 although it was tempered by the shock of seeing 'Mother and sister...at the door but I did not recognise them at first, they were both so very thin. My Mum had been such a tubby lady; now she seemed just a frail little woman.'

Many of the refugees had permanent jobs by this time and were satisfactorily housed. Nevertheless it was sometimes difficult to decide whether to go back. Ted Hocquard, who had had his own electrical business in St Helier in 1940, was offered an appointment as Works Manager when his company opened a new factory in Oxford. Late in 1945 he took a trip to Jersey to recover what he could of his furniture and to sell his house. Nothing of his Jersey business remained so he decided that his future lay in England. But even children who were quite young when they left the island of their birth retained a sense of belonging to and therefore being interested in the place where they were brought up. Ted Hocquard's daughter Margaret (now Mrs Newman) who was only seven when she evacuated says, 'It is strange but I still regard myself as a Jerseywoman even though I have not lived there for 54 years and we have only a few cousins with whom we keep in touch at Christmas.'

The schools too returned to Guernsey during the summer but only children who had homes in Guernsey were allowed to travel. In the case of Elizabeth College, the Head, the Rev. Milnes, made a special visit to the island to inspect the college building and to discuss with States officials what arrangements could be made for the return. The building had been occupied by Germans and was now in use by the British army. After overcoming various difficulties, plans were made for the return journey to be made on 1 August. A special train took the boys, as well as some of the parents who had obtained permission to return with the College, from Buxton to Southampton where they were addressed by Sir Donald Banks and the Mayor of Southampton, Councillor R. Stranger before boarding the *Hantonia*. The College reopened in Guernsey on 5 October.

The Ladies College at Denbigh, consisting of 31 girls and three teachers, Miss Ellershaw, Miss Bateson and Miss Syvret, also returned early in August. Some of the parents who lived in England joined them on 3 August and it was an excited party that set off by train for London on that day. The *Hantonia* was due to leave Southampton on the following day so they spent the night in a hostel near Waterloo station and had time to see something of London in the morning.

For some of the foster parents the parting was not a happy one. An Oldham family remembered:

> We took George to get on the coach outside school. I had kitted him out with new shirts, trousers, etc. and thought he looked really smart. When we had taken him in years before, I never thought for a minute how hard it would be for us to let him go. We had no children of our own and he felt like ours. Many of the boys were quite subdued. We waved as long as we could and then turned and walked down Chamber Road. Neither of us could speak, we were too upset. When we got to Star Inn my husband said, "Let's go to the pictures," and we went in the Gaumont. I don't know what we saw, but we couldn't go home you see, his little room seemed so empty.

For many of the children, now five years older, it was strange to be leaving the northern countryside that had become so familiar and especially to meet their real parents again. One boy wrote later:

Good-bye to the sheep, black cows, trains and double-decker buses; all new to us when we arrived in 1940. We took back with us strange accents, mostly Lancashire, with a smattering of Cheshire Derby and Welsh. But most of all we took back to Guernsey memories of family life, warmth and the love which had been showered on us for five years.

When we came back our families were all assembled at the Grammar school. It was very emotional. One thing I can remember, it was embarassing to call my own mother 'Mum'. It was five years away that had done this and it took me ages to return to a familiar footing.

W. A. Bisson who evacuated from Jersey with his mother and his aunt when he was nine, and now lives in Derbyshire, writes,

I have only been back to Jersey a few times on holidays but to me it will always be home. I can still remember quite clearly as a child watching the planes from England landing on the beach at West Park, fishing off St Catherine's breakwater, going on the train from St Helier to St Aubin, going for the day to St Brelade or Corbiere, seeing the Bretons in the tomato season in their national costumes in Hilgrove Street, or 'French Lane' as we called it.

Alderney

The return to Alderney, which had been almost completely evacuated by its population of 1,500, was more difficult. It was complicated by the fact that there was no local civil administration in the battered and much abused island after British forces returned there on 16 May 1945. On 11 August the Home Secretary set up a committee to enquire into the resettlement of the island. On 16 November the surviving members of the States of Alderney, still with Judge French as head, met in London to plan the resettlement in detail and on 2 December Judge French returned with a small party of former residents. More islanders were brought back during the month until by the end of 1945 there were 360 on the island. A few more returned during 1946 but by December of that year there was still only a third of the pre-war population in the island.

The resettlement did not go smoothly. Judge French seems to have become more and more autocratic and there were bitter arguments with residents. Finally he resigned in 1947 at the early age of 57. Just before this he was quoted in a Guernsey newspaper as saying, 'The reason for my resignation is this: that I led the people from the island at the evacuation in 1940. On four separate occasions while they were on the mainland I gave them my promise that I would do my best to see them safe back home. They are back home. My promise is fulfilled. The moral responsibility that I bore has been discharged. My work for the island has been done.'

He continued to live in the island during his retirement and died in 1962.

Appreciation

In the months following the Liberation, several CI societies made presentations to their host towns in grateful appreciation of the hospitality the refugees had received. Rochdale's Town Hall still displays the plaque presented in 1945 which reads 'Presented to the County Borough of Rochdale by resident Channel Islanders between 1940-1945 for many services rendered.'

The Bristol CI Society presented a model cider press to the city and in Exeter a plaque with the shields of the islands was presented at the Guildhall to the Mayor on 7 July 1945.

1940 – 1945

MEMBERS OF THE
CHANNEL ISLANDS SOCIETY
WHO MET IN THIS ROOM
DURING THEIR EXILE FROM HOME
Presented this Plaque in sincere appreciation
of kindness and friendship shown.

Plaque at Central Methodist Church, Nantwich.

The Aftermath

The removal of Guernsey children left a gap in the Guernsey community which is still felt. Several correspondents have mentioned that as teenagers after the war they felt a sense of guilt because almost as soon as they returned they wanted to go back to the UK, and within a couple of years had abandoned their parents. Others never had an opportunity to go back. Beryl Cox said (see Chapter 4) that she always yearned to go back to live in Jersey but was never able to. It was a cloud hanging over the whole of her adult life. This is typical of the feelings of many evacuees and accounts partly for the fact that in recent years many have returned to live in the islands on retirement.

On the other hand a number of correspondents, particularly those who were boys of 12 or upwards, have mentioned that they were very glad they evacuated. They felt at the time that it was a grand adventure. The experiences broadened their outlook and many had an early start in careers which put them well ahead of contemporaries who had remained in the islands during the occupation. Another correspondent told the author that when he was at school in Oldham he thinks the teachers pressed him to do better so that he would not let the side down: the evacuees from the CIs did not want to seem less able than their English contemporaries. He believes that because of this he was successful in obtaining a scholarship to Victoria College after the war.

'In retrospect it is perfectly clear that the Channel Islands should have been wholly evacuated,' says Norman Longmate in his book *How We Lived Then* (1971). Not every Channel Islander would agree with this. With hindsight many wished later they had remained in their homes. Property in Alderney, for example, would not have suffered so much loss and damage if the bulk of the population had remained, as they did in Sark. If Jersey and Guernsey had been completely evacuated it is likely that the Germans would have brought in large numbers of civilian foreigners as replacements and after the war the problems of rehabilitation would have been far greater than they were.

Those who criticise the decisions made in June 1940 must remember that the situation people found themselves in, either as individuals or administrators, was unprecedented and extremely complex. There might have been mass starvation or atrocities. The war might have lasted much longer than it did. The overcrowded and unprotected ships crossing the channel might have been attacked by the enemy. The fact that leading citizens in all four islands differed in their conclusions is an indication that at the time the decision to stay put or to flee was a gamble. Some regretted their decision, whichever way it went. Others believed later that they had done the right thing.

The Channel Islands

At this time of our liberation we desire to express our heartfelt thanks to all those hospitable and generous friends in the United Kingdom, in the Empire, and in the United States of America who, for nearly five years, have sheltered and helped our fellow islanders who left their homes immediately before the occupation of our islands by the enemy.

We have learnt through broadcasts, Red Cross messages, and letters from prisoners of war and from deportees of the warmth of the welcome given to our kinsfolk and of the unbounded kindness shown to them at all times and in all ways. The hearts of our fellow-islanders are, we know, like ours, filled with joy at the prospect of an early reunion, but they have made new friends whom they will never forget and to whom they and we owe a debt which we shall never be able to repay.

Victor G. Carey, Bailiff of Guernsey & A.M. Coutanche,
Bailiff of Jersey (letter in The Times 22 May 1945)

JERSEY		GUERNSEY

THE
CHANNEL ISLANDS
MONTHLY REVIEW

Journal of Channel Islands Refugees in Great Britain

PUBLISHED BY THE STOCKPORT AND DISTRICT
CHANNEL ISLANDS SOCIETY AT BOROUGH
CHAMBERS 1, ST. PETERSGATE, STOCKPORT

ALDERNEY		SARK

Vol. 8. No. 6. 24 Pages.	JUNE 1945	Price 4d.

LIBERATION

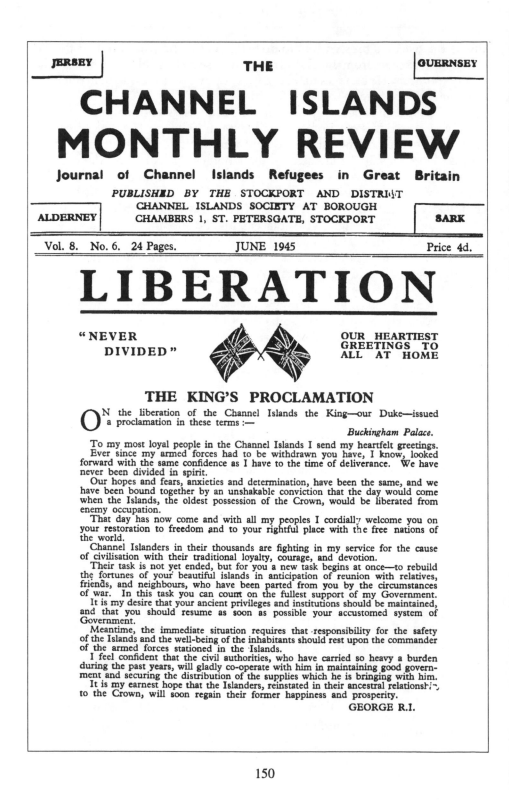

"NEVER
DIVIDED"

OUR HEARTIEST
GREETINGS TO
ALL AT HOME

THE KING'S PROCLAMATION

ON the liberation of the Channel Islands the King—our Duke—issued a proclamation in these terms :—

Buckingham Palace.

To my most loyal people in the Channel Islands I send my heartfelt greetings.

Ever since my armed forces had to be withdrawn you have, I know, looked forward with the same confidence as I have to the time of deliverance. We have never been divided in spirit.

Our hopes and fears, anxieties and determination, have been the same, and we have been bound together by an unshakable conviction that the day would come when the Islands, the oldest possession of the Crown, would be liberated from enemy occupation.

That day has now come and with all my peoples I cordially welcome you on your restoration to freedom and to your rightful place with the free nations of the world.

Channel Islanders in their thousands are fighting in my service for the cause of civilisation with their traditional loyalty, courage, and devotion.

Their task is not yet ended, but for you a new task begins at once—to rebuild the fortunes of your beautiful islands in anticipation of reunion with relatives, friends, and neighbours, who have been parted from you by the circumstances of war. In this task you can count on the fullest support of my Government.

It is my desire that your ancient privileges and institutions should be maintained, and that you should resume as soon as possible your accustomed system of Government.

Meantime, the immediate situation requires that responsibility for the safety of the Islands and the well-being of the inhabitants should rest upon the commander of the armed forces stationed in the Islands.

I feel confident that the civil authorities, who have carried so heavy a burden during the past years, will gladly co-operate with him in maintaining good government and securing the distribution of the supplies which he is bringing with him.

It is my earnest hope that the Islanders, reinstated in their ancestral relationship to the Crown, will soon regain their former happiness and prosperity.

GEORGE R.I.

Appendix A

Channel Islands Societies (See Chapter 8)

The following local societies are known to have been formed in Britain during the war. Other wartime Channel Islands societies were in Australia, Canada, Gibraltar, India, Malta and South Africa.

None appears to have survived later than 1950. The only two societies in the UK today with a general Channel Island interest are *The Jersey Society in London* and *The Guernsey Society* (also based in London).

Andover & District Channel Islands Society
Barnsley Channel Islands Society
Barnstable Channel Islands Society
Bath Channel Islands Society
Birmingham & District Channel Islands Society
Blackpool & Fylde Channel Islands Society
Bolton & District Channel Islands Society
Bournemouth & District Channel Islands Society
Bradford Channel Islands Society
Bradford Channel Islands Social Club
Bridgwater & District Channel Islanders' Society
Brighouse Channel Islands Society
Bristol Channel Islanders' Association
Burnley & District Channel Islands Society
Bury & District Channel Islands Society
Cardiff & District Channel Islands Society
Cathcart (Glasgow) Channel Islands Fellowship Circle
Chelmsford Channel Islands Society
Coventry & District Channel Islanders' Society
Croydon & East Surrey Channel Islands Society
Denbigh CI Society
Derby & Derbyshire Society of Channel Islanders
Devizes Channel Islands Society
Doncaster & District Channel Islands Society
Dunstable & District Channel Islands Society
Edinburgh & District Channel Islands Society
Exeter & District Channel Islanders' Society
Glasgow Sarnia Fellowship Circle
Glasgow Scottish Channel Islands Society
Glasgow Channel Islands Knitting Circle
Gloucester & District Channel Islands Society
Gosport Channel Islands Society
Guildford & District Channel Islands Society
Halifax Sarnia Club
Halifax Guernsey Society

Hampstead & District Channel Islands Society
Hereford & District Channel Islands Society
High Wycombe & District Channel Islands Society
Horsforth (Leeds) Channel Islands Society
Huddersfield Channel Islands Society
Isle of Wight Channel Islands Society
Kent, Channel Islanders Society of,
Kingston-upon-Thames Channel Islands Society
Leicester Channel Islands Society
Leicester & District Society of Channel Islanders
Lewisham Channel Islands Society
Lincoln & District Channel Islands Society
Manchester & District Channel Islands Society
Nantwich & District Channel Islands Society
Newbury & District Channel Islands Society
Newcastle-on-Tyne North-Eastern Channel Islands Association
Newquay (Cornwall) Channel Islands Fellowship
North London Channel Islands Society
North of England Federation of Channel Islands Societies
Nottingham & District Channel Islands Society
Oxford Channel Islands Society
Penzance and District Channel Islands Society
Plymouth & District Channel Islands Society
Poole & District Channel Islands Society
Port Talbot Channel Islands Society
Portsmouth & District Channel Islands Society
Reading & District (formerly Berkshire) Channel Islands Association
Richmond Channel Islands Society
Rochdale Guernsey & Jersey Social Club
Rochdale & District Channel Islands Society (formerly Guernsey Club)
Rothwell Channel Islands Society
Salisbury & District Channel Islands Society
Sheffield Channel Islands Society
Slough & Windsor Channel Islands Society
Southampton & District Channel Islands Association
St Albans & District Channel Islands Society
St. Helen's Channel Islands Society
Stockport & District Channel Islands Society
Streatham Hill & District Channel Islands Society
Swansea & District Channel Islanders Society
Swindon & District Channel Islands Society
Taunton & District Channel Islands Society
Tiverton Channel Islands Society
Wakefield & District Channel Islands Society
Wembley & District Channel Islands Society
Weymouth & District Channel Islands Society
Wigan Channel Islands Circle
Wolverhampton & District Channel Islanders' Society
Woolwich Channel Islands Society

Appendix B

Guernsey Schools

Name of School[1]	Staff in U.K.[1]	No.[2]	Location in UK[3]
Amherst			Glasgow
Castel School	Miss A.E. Ninnim	162	Clonastin, Ollerton, Knutsford, Cheshire
Convent, Alderney			pupils to Alderley Edge, Cheshire
St Sampson's	Sister M. de Sales O'Connor	135	Wharton Road, Winsford, Cheshire
Elizabeth College (Juniors)	Major W.C.F. Caldwell	60	Great Hucklow, Derbys.
Elizabeth College (Seniors)	Revd. W.H.G. Milnes, Dorothy I.E. Cumber, Eric Chambers, R. Shaw	105	Whitehall, Buxton, Derbys.
Forest & St. Martin's	Mr. P. Martel	132	Parish Hall, Cheadle Hulme, Cheshire
Hautes Capelles Infants	Miss M. Falla	44	Spurstow Council School, Tarporley, Cheshire
Hautes Capelles Junior	Miss W. Bisson, Miss C. Martel	51	Bunbury C. of E. School, Tarporley, Cheshire, Church School Bickerton, Malpas, Cheshire
Kermaria School, L'Islet	Sister Pierre Fourier (G. Nael), Sister Anthony (Z. Morin), Sister Timothy (Marie J. Joly)	35	St. Peter's Hall, Hazel Grove, Cheshire
Ladies College	Miss Ellershaw	30	Howell's School, Denbigh, N. Wales
Les Cotils			
Les Eturs Infant School, Castel	Miss F.E. Duchemin	2	Wicham C. of E. School, Northwich, Cheshire
Les Vauxbelets College	Revd. Bro. M.C. Benoistel, Charles Clews Aquilina, Bro. J.F. Boylan, E. Conlon, Bro. H.C. Danielov, B. Fricker, E. Heumann, M. Le Corre, D. McDonagh	21	St. Ambrose's College, Altrincham, Cheshire
Notre Dame du Rosaire	Sister M. Gautier, Miss I.C. Green, M. Galten, V.A. Valentine, M.J. Provost, E.M. Meagher	20+	Holly Mount, Tottington, Bury
St. Andrew's			Irby and Barnston Women's Institute
St Anne's, Alderney			Alderley Edge, Cheshire

St. Joseph's	Sister Patricia, V. Kreckeler, M. Hudson, B. Adams	23	St. Martin's Hall, Marple, Cheshire
St. Martin's Boys	Miss Kathleen Clarke	33	Oughtrington Council School, Lymm, Lancashire
St. Martin's Girls	Miss Amelia Page Page Baker	27	C. of E. School, Richmond Road, Bowden, Cheshire
St Peter in the Wood (Juniors), St Pierre du Bois	H. Brelsford	30	Disley Secondary Modern, Disley, Cheshire
St Peter in the Wood (Seniors), St Pierre du Bois	Walter C. Brehaut, Mrs Mildred Smith	42	Haworth Senior School, Keighley, Yorkshire
St. Saviour's Mixed	G.A. Vining	21	The Institute, Neston, Cheshire
States Intermediate (Boys)	F.E. Fulford	141	Hulme Grammar School, Oldham
States Intermediate (Girls)	Miss Roughton	23	Boothroyde, Manchester Road, Rochdale
The Children's Home, Castel	Harry Brown (Manager) Mrs V. Brown (Matron) Mrs O.M. Brouard (nurse) Mrs D. G. Lainé (cook) Mrs M.L. Hantonne (nurse) Lena G. Le Poidevin (nurse)	83	Danesmoor, Bury
The Froebel School, St Peter Port	Miss M. Wilson Barnett	21	Froebel School, Ardvorlich, Loch Earnhead
Torteval School	F.H. Le Poidevin	62	Alderley Edge Council School, Ryley's Lane, Manchester
Vale Infants	Miss E. Le Poidevin, Miss F.E. Duchemin	12	Audlem C of E Junior School, Crewe
Vale Junior	Mrs Hampton, Miss Enid Corbet, R.E. Carré, Mrs M.V. Mahy	79	Buerton Council School Wrenbury, Nantwich, Worleston C. of E. School, Nantwich

No information relating to the following schools has come to light during the research for this list: Blancheland, Burnt Lane, Cordier Hill, Delancey High School, Kingsley House, La Chaumiere, Les Cotils, Morely, Saward, Sorel, St. Sampson's and Vauvert.

1. Few official records have survived in Guernsey. These names are taken mainly from wartime records made in the UK in 1994 and from private correspondence. The list of teachers is incomplete.

2. There is no known record of the numbers which evacuated with each school. Many children left school, or moved elsewhere, in 1941-44.

3. The pupils of some Guernsey schools were divided among two or more schools in the UK.

Sources and Bibliography

Jersey Society in London, Archives.

Société Jersiaise. Occupation papers; Channel Islands Refugees Committee and Alderney Relief Committee, Annual Reports, 1940-45.

Public Record Office. Home Office papers (Files HO144-22829, 22830,22831).

Women's Royal Voluntary Services Archives (London). Papers on CI refugees.

BBC Written Archives, Caversham.

Mrs Eliz. Downer & Miss Anne Nichol. Diaries & drawings of Diana Falla.

Bury Records Office. File ABU/T/792.

Oldham Museum: 'Guernsey Boys' exhibition, 1990.

Mr K. Renault. Minutes and letter books of the Gosport CI Society.

Post Office Archives, London.

Acutt, D.G.F., *Brigade in Action*, Weymouth, 1946.

Attwooll, M & Harrison, D., *Weymouth & Portland at War*, Dovecote Press, 1993.

Bonnard, Brian, *Alderney at War, 1939-49*, Alan Sutton, 1993.

Buckfield, Miss J. E., *The History of the Guernsey Ladies College 1872-1963*, Guernsey Press, 1965.

Colenette, V.G., *Elizabeth College in Exile*, Guernsey Press, n.d.

Collenette, V., *Elizabeth College*, Guernsey, 1965.

Cortvriend, V.V., Isolated Island, Guernsey Star & Gazette, 1947.

Cottrill, D. J., *Victoria College Jersey, 1852-1972*, Phillimore, 1977.

Cruickshank, C., *The German Occupation of the Channel Islands*, Oxford University Press, 1975.

Durand, Ralph, *Guernsey under German Rule*, The Guernsey Society, 1946.

Edwards, G.B., *The Book of Ebenezer Le Page*, H. Hamilton, 1981.

Gurney, David, *The Red Cross Civilian Postal Message Scheme with the Channel Islands*, C.I.S.S., 1992.

Hamel, E.J., *X-Iles*, Guernsey Press, 1975.

Inglis, Ruth, *The Children's War – Evacuation 1939-1945*, Collins, 1989.

Keeling, A. R. *Written in Exile: a collection of verse* , Penzance, 1945.

Le Pelley, P., The Evacuation of Guernsey Schoolchildren: *Channel Islands Occupation Review*, (1988) Channel Islands Occupation Society.

Le Ruez, Nan, *Jersey Occupation Diary*, Seaflower Books, 1994.

Longmate, N., *How We Lived Then*, Hutchinson, 1971.

Marshall, Michael, *The Small Army*, Constable, 1957.

McKenzie, Donald, *The Red Cross Mail Service for CI Civilians, 1940-45*, Picton Publishing, Chippenham, 1975.

Millett, Freda, *Oldham and its People*, Oldham Leisure Services n.d.

Picot, D. et al., *War Memoirs of a Jersey Family*, Jersey, 1993.

Quin, Olive, *The Long Goodbye*, Guernsey Press, 1985.

Read, B.A., *Jersey in London*, Seaflower Books, 1994.

Russell, Yvonne, *A Guernsey Girl Evacuee joins the W.A.A.F. in Wartime England*, Toucan Press, Guernsey , 1988.

Sinel, Leslie, *Occupation Diary*, Jersey 1945.

Vatcher, H.M., 'The Royal Militia Island of Jersey', *Annual Bulletin Soc. Jersiaise*, 1951.

Wadsworth, John, *Counter Defensive*, Hodder & Stoughton, 1946.

Evening Post (Jersey).

Evening Press (Guernsey),

The Channel Islands Monthly Review (Stockport 1941-45).

Index

158

JERSEY RAMBLES
by John Le Dain
This book describes the routes of 28 rambles, from easy twenty-minute strolls to longer, more demanding rambles.
All aspects of the Jersey landscape are included here, from the rugged and magnificent north coast to the gentler charms of the island's well-wooded, south-sloping valleys.
128 pages; Pen & ink drawings plus 28 maps, Price £4.95

THE JERSEY LILY
by Sonia Hillsdon
Born Emilie Le Breton in Jersey in 1853, married to Edward Langtry at the age of twenty, Lillie Langtry was destined to be universally known as 'The Jersey Lily', the most beautiful woman in the world.
128 pages; fully illustrated; Price £4.95
'This book is thorough, well-written and entertaining.' – *The Jersey Society in London Bulletin.*

JERSEY: NOT QUITE BRITISH
by David Le Feuvre
This book is about an island, its history, its culture and its people. The author outlines events which helped to form the special character of the men and women who were Jersey's original inhabitants.
'This is gripping reading, colourful, proud and sad. It is not only an enlightening and entertaining work, but also an important one, whose author has done Jersey an enduring service by vividly conveying and recording the true nature of what is lost.' – *Jersey Evening Post.*
160 pages; illustrated; Price £5.95

JERSEY IN LONDON
by Brian Ahier Read
In 1895 a lone Jerseyman in London arranged a meeting with friends from Jersey who worked in the city. *Jersey in London* tells the story of how that small group of expatriates grew into a flourishing organisation. Its members have included some of the most eminent Jersey people of the century. For the Jersey historian this book offers a unique insight into a hitherto little known aspect of real Jersey folk and members of some well-known local families.
192 pages; illustrated; fully indexed; Price £6.95

JERSEY OCCUPATION DIARY
Her story of the German Occupation, 1940-45
by Nan Le Ruez
'Now a new book has been added to the list of those which speak accurately, candidly and with authority about the Occupation ... As well as painting a comprehensive picture of the daily round of drudgery which was necessary to run the farm and keep everyone fed and clothed in those most trying of times, the diary is also a record of more personal suffering ... Anyone who reads this account is likely to be impressed by its directness, its clarity and the depth of feeling it reveals ...'

from a review in the Jersey Evening Post.
304 pages; pencil drawings, photographs and map; Price £9.95

THE MOTOR CAR IN JERSEY
by David Scott Warren
Just about every aspect of Jersey's century-long association with the motor car is included here. The author's text is informed by considerable knowledge of the subject as well as by an unmistakable enthusiasm, and is supported by an interesting and wide-ranging collection of pictures.
128 pages; over 60 photographs; Price £6.95

LIFE ON SARK
by Jennifer Cochrane
What is it really like to live in a small island community? Most holiday-makers to Sark are day visitors during the summer season – the impression they gain is very different to the reality of the winter months and the rest of the year.
This well informed and fondly written book is guaranteed to delight anyone intrigued by this island gem, which is perhaps the Channel Island with the greatest mystique.
128 pages; 42 black & white photographs; 12 pencil drawings; map; Price £4.95

SEAFLOWER BOOKS may be obtained through local bookshops or direct from the publishers, post-free, on receipt of net price, at:

1 The Shambles, Bradford on Avon, Wiltshire, BA15 1JS
Tel/ Fax 01225 863595

Please ask for our free, illustrated list.